AF478179

Cultural Sociology within Innovative Treatise

Islamic Insights on Human Symbols

Mahmoud Dhaouadi

University Press of America,® Inc.
Lanham • Boulder • New York • Toronto • Plymouth, UK

Library of Congress Control Number: 2013930941
ISBN: 978-0-7618-5922-2 (cloth : alk. paper)—ISBN: 978-0-7618-5923-9 (electronic)

∞™ The paper used in this publication meets the minimum requirements of American National Standard for Information Sciences Permanence of Paper for Printed Library Materials, ANSI/NISO Z39.48-1992.

To the revolting people of the Arab World:

While I am finishing the editing of this book, Tunisians, Egyptians, Lybians and Yemenites have successfully revolted against their presidents, their regimes and their ruling parties. Also, I can only greet the other continuing Arab uprising in Syria and I hope they all constitute real promising signs for establishing a true new culture which can secure authentic identities, democracy, freedom of expression and equality between the citizens and the countries' regions. The study of Human Symbols/HS in this work may well fall within the revolutionary spirit the Arab uprisings. I examine HS in this book with innovative vision and new conceptualization which are hardly found in the epistemology of modern social sciences.

Ezzahra, Tunisia: March 22, 2012.

Contents

Preface

First, this book is a basic introduction to the universe of *Human Symbols* (HS): language, thought, religion, knowledge/science, myths, cultural values and norms. The study of HS is strongly related to the promotion of cultural sociology. The latter is a young growing branch of modern sociology. That is, the chapters of this treatise constitute a genuine introduction which seeks to establish many important foundations of cultural sociology whose late coming is attributed to the negligence of the study of culture by the founding Fathers of western sociology. This explains the almost complete absence of the role of culture in the making of their sociological thought with its various concepts and theories. As such, the core text of this work could be considered first as an intellectual contribution to push forward the process of the development of cultural sociology, through wide and fundamental explorations of the universe of HS.

On the one hand, I present in the first chapter of this book my own independent research way in the exploration of the horizons of cultural sociology. On the other hand, I put forward my criticism of current cultural sociology particularly its lack of acknowledging the presence of what I call 'transcendental features' of my concept of HS/culture. What is meant by the adjective 'transcendental' in this treatise is that HS have neither weight nor volume in the material sense of the word. Thus, the essential nature of HS is rather spiritual and not materialistic.

I emphasize in this book that the discovery of transcendental features and other dimensions of the universe of HS is a basic introduction in favour of establishing a cultural sociology with solid credibility.

Second, I believe that the content of the book's chapters is a mere beginning/introduction to the vast and complex universe of HS to which cultural sociology pays a great attention. In my own perspective, cultural sociology focuses its basic research on what I have already called HS which gives the human race domination over the rest of the species. Thus, the sailing into the deep knowledge system of the nature of HS and their impact on the behaviors of the human individuals and the dynamics of human societies represent a legitimate introduction to unveil certain features of the enormous and intricate universe of HS.

The building of a credible scientific and reliable human knowledge on HS could be seen as the top of all human knowledge related to the understanding and explanation of people's behaviours and the movements of their societies. Consequently, research in the field of HS can only be a very wide one and perhaps without frontiers. Philosophers, social thinkers and other scholars interested in the study of human behavior consider *Man as a big puzzle* on this planet. Attempts to secure vast knowledge on the human species deserve, therefore, full legitimacy. Thus, the beginning of establishing a genuine corpus of knowledge on Man should start from the ABC knowledge of HS which represent the main keys to have deep access to a vertical and horizontal knowledge that can strongly help understand and explain the special phenomena of Man and human society. There are practically no limits to such knowledge adventure in HS which distinguishes most the human race and give it an overwhelming superiority over the other species.

The potential contribution of this accumulated knowledge harvest on HS in the book's chapters is a primary introduction to unveil the hidden as well as the transcendental features of HS. As a dominant perspective in science and knowledge, Positivism's ethics hardly pays attention to these aspects of HS which my treatise's chapters stress their great importance.

Third, my research on HS since 1990s has led me in an almost fully independent way to *new visions and concepts in the HS universe*. This may resemble on one level the way Ibn Khaldun had discovered his New Science in his Muqaddimah The book's first chapter describes my road map to cultural sociology. The one level similarity between Ibn Khaldun's Muqaddimah and my work in this book is confined to the assumption that both works put forward new perspectives for understanding and explaining the phenomena in question. The author of the Muqaddimah had established a new science to understand and explain the events and the social phenomena of human civilization and social organization in the Arab Muslim world in particular. The corpus of my own explorations of the HS universe in this book offers plenty of fair new insights, concepts and theoretical frameworks relevant to dealing and studying the universe HS/culture. As it will be shown in the book's chapters, I may claim that Western young cultural sociology hardly mentions, let alone analyses and discusses, those new features which are outlined by my new sociological cultural framework. I like to underline here only few new intellectual tools that distinguish my HS cultural sociology from the Western one, especially in the USA. I mention and explain in the following some of the new aspects that my research in the HS/culture universe has come to explore and discover:

1-The basic research of my thesis in the explorations of the HS universe strongly claims that *humans* are profoundly *cultural beings by nature* . That is, the essence of human nature is first and for most cultural symbolic one. HS are, thus, the first determining forces of human identity. In other words, the role of HS/culture in shaping the aspects of the identity of the human species' is a central prominent role. This epistemological view of the cultural symbolic nature of human nature hardly finds a similar one among the perspectives and the theories of contemporary social sciences like Marxism, Structural-Functionalism, Behaviorism, Psychoanalysis and even Symbolic Interaction. Unlike this book's thesis, these dominant schools in social sciences do not give a prior central role to the influence of HS on the shaping of human identity and action. This is quite different from this work's position which points out with full clarity and transparency that humans are fully cultural beings. Such an intellectual vision has grown and matured after many years of intellectual reflections to become a genuine theory as shown in more than one chapter of this book.

2-This new conceptualization of the symbolic cultural nature of humans finds – through my similar interpretive Geertz approach to the Quran text - strong support which I do not encounter in the discourse of past and modern Interpreters (Al Mufassirun) of the Quran. Al Mufassirun give a common meaning to the word (My sprit: Ruhi) in the verse where God asks the angels to bow to Adam: (I am about to create man, from sounding clay from mud moulded into shape. When I have fashioned him (in due proportion) and breathed into him of My Spirit, fall ye down in obeisance into him (The Quran 15:28-29). The common meaning adopted by Al Mufassirun for 'My Spirit' is the infusion of life/soul in the human being. I see such a meaning is hardly in harmony with the context of the verse in question. This verse calls upon the angels to prostrate only to Adam after God's Spirit had been infused in him. It must be known that the word Spirit (Ruh) has various meanings in the text of the Quran. If the meaning of the word My Spirit means the mere infusion of life in living beings, God's call on the angels to prostrate would not be restricted only to Adam. Consequently, there must be a different meaning to the word (*Ruhi: My Spirit*) which is fully compatible with the context of the Quran's verse. This different meaning of the word (My Spirit) should be, in my opinion, those *special human traits* which have given Adam/Man strong legitimacy to receive the angels' prostration and to have the overwhelming domination (to be the Master/Khalifa) over the other living beings in the world.

My analysis in this treatise shows that HS are the only determinant forces which have enabled humans to be dominant in this world. As such, the meaning of the word (My Spirit) in the verse should/must mean first of all the HS/culture. As far as I know, this kind of interpretation of the word 'My Spirit' is something **new** which is not referred to in the books of the Interpreters of the Quran throughout the centuries. The compatibility between the meaning of the HS and that of the word (My Spirit) in the verse is a sort of methodology which combines both the use of reason (Aql) and reliance on sacred knowledge (Naql). The authentic traditional learned intellectual Islamic knowledge/ science is well known for this type of methodology which Ibn Khaldun, among past Muslim scholars and scientists, had adopted in writing his pioneering famous Muqaddimah in the social sciences. Based on matching HS with the divine Spirit, one could find, for example, an explanation for the long lifespan or to the potential eternity of the HS various manifestations or for what makes human thought, languages, religious beliefs, scientific ideas (as essential components of HS) prone to last for thousands of years or may be for semi- eternity.

A legitimate answer to this question could be offered by the above view that sees HS as being derived from the divine eternal Spirit. In other words, HS have certain aspects of the divine nature including the very long/potential eternal existence. Contemporary social sciences hardly reflect on the long lifespan of HS in human societies and civilizations, let alone providing an explanation to it. Consequently, this Islamic epistemology of the correspondence between HS ant the divine Spirit grants a sound account to the very long duration survival of HS. To my knowledge, this could be considered a new insight very relevant to the understanding of the nature of culture/HS as well as to the study of its dynamics which have preoccupied especially anthropologists, cultural sociologists and sociologists in the contemporary period.

3-As to the *new* third feature which I have discovered through my concept of the centrality of HS/culture in the identity of humans, it has to do with my explanation of the slow human body growth as well as the human longer lifespan, in comparison with those of other living beings. As stressed before, HS distinguish the human species. I use HS to explain the two human characteristics just mentioned. The following example shows the credibility of this assumption. On the one hand, we know that the human babies can walk on average a little before or a little after reaching one year of age. On the other hand, animal babies are able to walk at birth or after only few hours or days after their birth. I found that the cause of the walking delay among human babies could be attributed to HS. I explain the link between HS and the human walking delay in more than one chapter in this work. I believe that the discovery of this link is something *new* whose truth is hardly given credit by common people as well as by most learned men and women. In fact, I have noticed wide astonishment and perplexity among all of them toward the potential existing link between human babies walking delay and the HS. Ibn Khaldun's terms in speaking about his invention of his New Science may be relatively fit to be applied on the link in question here: "It should be known that the discussion of this topic (the link between HS and human babies walking delay here) is something new and extraordinary..."(Ibn Khaldun 1974: 39).

Fourth, another new feature which I have come to discover through my assumption of the HS centrality in human identity is displayed in my new conceptualization of the dual identity of humans. Philosophers, religious men and women and the general public often think of humans as made of body and soul. On my part, I think that I have made a new contribution to the traditional conceptualization of that dual human identity, so I believe it has become *more transparent.* The human common knowledge of the real essence of the human soul is much short of clarity. Consequently, I see fit to replace it by HS in the analysis of the dual human identity. That is, in my perspective the nature of the human dual entity has become: body and HS instead of body and soul. Very likely, this may constitute an *innovative* frame for the charting of the dual human identity. This new insightful outlook should promote more transparency as far as the making of the human identity is concerned. As such, it should enable us more to understand as well as to explain the interaction of the two poles (body and HS) of the human identity and the impact of that on human behaviors of individuals as well as the various patterns of human societies and civilizations' dynamics.

Fifth, as mentioned earlier, my focused research in the layers of HS (language, thought, religion, knowledge/science, myths, cultural values and norms...) has made me discover that they have *neither weight nor volume* in the material sense of things. That is to say, HS are not material elements. They are rather spiritual or transcendental. My description of HS as having no volume and no weight can be also considered 'something *new* and extraordinary' as Ibn Khaldun saw his New Science. This new non-materialist conceptualization of the HS universe has led me to identify certain characteristics and laws which distinguish the HS part from the body part in the human dual identify. For instance, our material goods and monetary capital will be reduced if we give some of them to others as a charity or a gift. While nothing is reduced or lost from our HS if we teach, for example, others our language, our knowledge/science or spread among them our religions beliefs. My new conceptualization of HS as having neither weight nor volume helps offer a new explanation, on the one hand, to the fast transmission of the spoken and the written word in the age of the Information Revolution and, on the other hand, this could explain as well the ability to put the enormous content – whose weight is many tons - of thousands of encyclopaedias, dictionaries, books, journals and newspapers in few Flash Disks. Chapter VI in particular will offer a detailed account on this matter from my perspective of HS. I think the science of HS/cultural sociology presented in this treatise could be considered a genuine basic reference that might deserve be consulted in order to understand and explain the single human individual's behaviours as well as the collective ones. I mention in this book that the knowledge provided by cultural sociology about humans and their societies is the core of all branches of human knowledge on them. Are not humans first of all cultural beings by nature?

The analysis presented here should give legitimacy to the use of the word *treatise* in the book's title. The chapters of this work attempt to establish new fresh insights and grounds in the universe of HS/culture which could promote our understanding and explanation of various individual and collective behaviors in human societies. In doing so, the status of cultural sociology is likely to be enhanced.

As for the meaning of 'the Universe of Human Symbols' in this book's title, it refers to new deep and global explorations of what distinguishes humans most from the other species. It has to do here with the HS universe. In my view, HS/culture constitutes a central dimension in the human identity as well as in human society. This outlook of HS/culture is different from what is called sociology of culture. The latter looks at culture/HS as a dependent variable, for instance, on economy and social structure of society. While my research efforts have focused from the start on the principal founding elements (HS) of cultural sociology and not on those of sociology of culture.

As far as the term Islamic in the book's title, it indicates that few of this treatise's chapters use the Islamic perspective and especially the Quranic one in the study as well as the analysis and discussion of the nature and the concept of culture in sociology and anthropology. Having explained all the terms of the book's title, I hope this would clarify the confusion which some of the words may create. In doing so, I believe the entire title of the book becomes clear both at the level of each word and at the level of the whole title.

REFERENCES

Khaldun, Ibn. (1974). *The Muqaddimah: An Introduction to History*. Dawood, N.J. (Ed.). (Franz Rosenthal, Trans.). Princeton Bolling Series: Princeton University Press.

I

New Conceptual Exploration into Cultural Sociology

Chapter One

The Search for Cultural Sociology

SOCIOLOGY OF CULTURE AND CULTURAL SOCIOLOGY

There is today a strong consensus that the study of culture by sociologists has been a late comer in the discipline of sociology. This is true both of the sociology of culture (Crane 1995) and cultural sociology (Spillman 2007). The former has been virtually reinvented since the early 1970s. Also cultural sociology has emerged since the 1990s with what is called 'the Cultural Turn' (Bonnell, Hunt 1999).

Although both the sociology of culture and cultural sociology have a commun conceptual repertoire, the former sees culture as a dependent variable while the latter treats it as an independent variable that possesses a relative autonomy in shaping both human action and social institutions.

The sociology of culture's new perspectives deal with the reinterpretation of perennial issues in sociological thought. That's is, how to define and conceptualize culture in all its contemporary ramifications, how to conceptualize the relationship between structure and culture and to conduct systematic studies of culture in its social context in a time when traditional notions of cause and effect no longer seem relevant (Crane 1995: 17).

On the other hand, cultural sociology is defined by Spillman as "about meaning – making". Cultural sociologists investigate how meaning-making happens, why meanings vary, how meanings influence human action, and why meaning-making is important in social cohesion, domination, and resistance" (Spillman 2007: 1).

The terms 'weak program' and 'strong program' are widely used today by cultural sociologists to distinguish sociology of culture from cultural sociology. Both recognize the importance of culture for society and appear to have a great deal in common. However, the apparent similarities are only superficial. The sociology of culture regards culture as something "soft" and dependent rather than a truly independent variable. In other words, in the sociology of culture, an "insignificant" role is assigned to culture and, as such, it is given a 'thin description', as the anthropologist Glifford Geertz would put it.

Within this outlook, the classical period (pre-1960) of the social theory of culture, including the sociologies of Weber, Durkheim, Marx, Parsons, Mills and others belong to the 'weak program'.

Furthermore, the modern (post-1960) period has at least four types of 'weak program': the Birmingham School, Bourdieu, Foucault and 'the theory of the production and consumption of culture'.

It should be emphasized here that the 'weak program' still dominates today the overall sociological studies of culture, even though cultural sociology of a 'strong program" is gaining ground especially in American sociology (Daloz, Erdemir, Semashko 2006: 829-838).

FLIRTING WITH THE DEVELOPMENT OF THEORETICAL SOCIAL SCIENCE PERSPECTIVE

On my part, my involvement in cultural sociology developed rather independently from my Western academic studies and readings in the social sciences.

First, my story with cultural sociology began around 1990s. My interest in this new branch of sociology took place in an indirect way. I was then flirting with the idea of establishing my own perspective or a paradigm or a theory which can help comprehend and explain both individual behaviours and the dynamics of human societies and civilizations.

Such a research goal required a suitable methodology that could put me on solid ground for this ambitious work of this treatise. I told myself that my best methodology would be *to chart,* so to speak, *those traits/characteristics* which radically and categorically distinguish the human race from other species and give it overwhelming domination over them. Because I assumed that a perspective, a paradigm or a theory which is based on fundamental human distinct traits/characteristics… would more likely qualify to be credible and reliable as far as understanding and explaining the behaviours of the individuals as well as the social dynamics of human societies and civilizations. In other words, I argued that the human distinct traits/characteristics must be *square one* where the social scientist should begin his/her work in attempting to build valid theoretical social science framework (a treatise) for the understanding and explanation of human affairs. Thus, a set of the human distinct traits/characteristics is considered to be the major key for seeking articulate understanding and explanation of what goes on in the human world.

HUMAN SYMBOLS ARE CENTRAL TO HUMAN IDENTITY

The comparative charting process of common and uncommon traits/characteristics between the human race and the other living species has led me to realize that the human race has certain features which the other species either do not have or they have a lower degree level of them. These are what I call *Human Symbols (HS)* spoken and written language, thought, religion, knowledge/science, myths, laws, cultural values and norms... My definition of HS is similar to that of culture of Edward B. Tylor "Culture, or civilization... is that complex whole which in includes knowledge, belief, art, morals, custom, and any other capacities and habits acquired by man as a member of society" (Encyclopedia of Sociology 1974:69).

Starting my enquiry for the understanding of humans and their societies from the basics of HS is seen as compatible with the concept of *'Return to Basics'*. Since HS are what distinguish humans most from the other species, they should; therefore, be seen to be the basics of human identity and of the action of human agency. Thus, the focus on studying the nature of HS becomes very legitimate for me, as a social scientist, in order to establish credible social scientific knowledge which offers good insights and reliable understanding and explanation to individual and collective human behaviours. Because HS are the most outstanding founding components of human identity, they can be looked at as very central to the making of human nature itself. This allows social scientists to say that the human race is by nature a symbolic race. HS strongly advocates that HS (culture) are independent and autonomous variables as would argue today cultural sociologists of the 'strong program' orientation.

THE LEGITIMACY OF RETURN TO BASICS

The focus on the study of HS is a strong stand in favour of the principle: Return to Basics adopted both by social and natural scientists like Noam Chomsky in his study of language and Edward Wilson in his invention of sociobiology.

On my part, the exploration in depth of HS is considered as a direct return to the very center of the human identity. As outlined before, HS are what distinguish radically humans from the other species and grant the former an overwhelming domination over the latter. *If Man* has always presented as *a puzzle* for philosophers, social thinkers and scientists as well, I consider HS as the first source through which we can come closer to the discovery and the understanding of that intriguing and mysterious puzzle. As such, the establishment of a treatise of a solid corpus of knowledge on HS would be classified as the core social scientific knowledge ever that is highly qualified to offer well grounded understanding and explanation of the behaviours of social actors and the dynamics of human societies and civilizations (Hoover 1988).

HUMANS THE GREAT HS USERS

My perspective's intense focus on Man's HS has led me to say "Humans are by nature cultural symbolic beings" before" being social by nature" as stated by philosophers and social thinkers of all times and civilizations. That is, Man possesses *a complex and unique high quality HS system* made of spoken and written language, cultural values and norms and the ability to use the symbols for making knowledge and science. Man also has high cognitive skills which allow for tangible and abstract thinking which may reach very complex and sophisticated levels. These examples and others of Man's intense and complex use of HS make Man legitimately qualified to be uniquely called the Homo Symbolicus, a new concept on which are based all the chapters of this treatise.

HUMANS ARE EXCELLENT HOMO SYMBOLICUS

Having observed that HS are special and unique characteristics of humans, let us see now how HS are deeply central in the human identity. That is, how humans are fully conceived first in this book as Homo Symbolicus. The latter quality is based on a set of five observations/concepts of my own:

1. The process of the human body growth and maturation is very slow compared with those of other living beings. For instance, on average human babies begin walking at the age of one year, while animal babies may walk at birth or within few hours or days after their birth.
2. In general, humans have longer lifespan than those of many animals.
3. The human race has a dominant role in this world.
4. Humans are privileged by what I already called HS: spoken and written language, thought, religion, knowledge/science, laws, myths, cultural values and norms…
5. The human identity is made up of two parts: the body and HS. As such, it is fully a dualistic identity which is often referred to in religion and philosophy as an identity made of body and soul.

As to the late walk of human babies, I sent an e-mail message to the Scientific American (SA) magazine asking specifically for an explanation of this late human babies walk. The SA editor has remained silent for about a year. I received the reply message, October 19, 2005, which had no answer to my question. The SA editor's message advised me only to search for possible answers to my question in anthropology's websites.

POTENTIAL EXPLANATION OF HS TO THE LATE HUMAN WALK

In the absence of SA scientific explanation to the late human babies walk phenomenon, I found myself as a researcher compelled to look for a potential explanatory hypothesis which stipulates the following:

The late walk of human babies could be accounted for by the fact that human global growth and maturation involve two fronts: The body front and the HS front. In short, the growth and maturation of non-human species are uni-dimensional. (That is, they predominantly involve the body) because of their major lack of HS in the most complex human sense of the term. In contrast, the growth and maturation of human are bi-dimensional. That is, they involve two levels: the body level and the HS level. So, the process of two levels is seen in my hypothesis to be behind the human slow body growth and maturation which lead, consequently, to late walk of human babies. This assumption is based on logical reasoning. Logical reasoning would conclude that the rapid body growth and maturation among the non-humans is assumed to be due to the uni-dimensional/body process of growth and maturation .While the slow body growth and maturation among humans is due to the fact that they go through two processes of growth and maturation. In logical reasoning terms, it takes longer time for the accomplishment of the two processes of growth and maturation to materialise than for just one single process. In other words, the process of human body growth and maturation is slowed down, so to speak, among humans because humans are involved in *a second process* of growth and maturation represented by HS.

Furthermore, the growth and maturation of HS appear to be by their own nature slower than the human body processes of growth and maturation. While the latter reach their peak of growth and maturation in the twenties (Rischer, Easton 1992:423), some features of HS reach their higher and highest stages of growth and maturation much later in human lifespan. For instance, humans could hardly reach, before the age of 40 years, the peak of growth and maturation in the fields of thought, religious experience and knowledge and science. This gives strong legitimacy to humans' strong need for longer lifespan as shown in the drawing below. In other words, the human longer lifespan could be seen as the outcome of the human double fronts of growth and maturation factor underlined above.

The human body growth and maturation peak in the twenties helps explain also two other features of human life:

1. Athletes are known to often retire after they reach the age of 25 years or so.
2. On the intellectual/thought level, humans can hardly manifest mature thinking before the twenties. This could be explained as follows: once humans have finished the business of their body growth and maturation in their twenties, they can now concentrate more, so to speak, on the development and maturation of their HS for the rest of their lives. This should explain as well why real high mature scientific theories and intellectual complex thought can hardly see the light before the age of 40 years.

The following drawing illustrates the centrality of the HS in the human identity. This gives legitimacy to my new conceptualization which stipulates that humans are by nature cultural symbolic beings. That is, HS are at the core of the human race's identity, because they strongly influence/determine the remaining four distinctive human features (1, 2, 3, 5) in the drawing below. In cultural sociology's terms, this would make my conceptualization a very ` strong program` culture oriented one. Since culture/HS are very central to its epistemology, its explanatory perspective and its theorizing about the behaviours of human individuals and the social dynamics of human societies. *HS* should, thus, qualify to be *an avant-garde vision for today emerging cultural sociology* (Spillman 2007).

Therefore, HS could explain the human body slow growth and maturation, the human longer lifespan, the dominant role humans play in the world and the human dual identity. In other words, HS centrality in the human identity helps explain different phenomena in the human world.

Furthermore, HS central position in the human entity as shown leads to the emergence of a new concept which is rather opposite to Sociobiology (Wilson 1975).The new concept is what I would like to call Bioculturology. The latter means that HS (the human cultural system) has an implicit determinant impact on the very given genetic design of the human body which is made to be slow in growth and maturation. It is assumed here that the slow body process in question is made so in order to meet the need of HS for a longer lifespan in order that they can be fully developed, grown and matured. This is consistent with the idea of the assumed influence of mind over matter or that of the psychological on the organic in humans (Pedler 1981).

HS TRANSCENDENTAL DIMENSIONS

Having identified first that HS are distinct features of humans and second that HS are central in the human identity, I wish thirdly to elaborate on my idea which stipulates that HS have what I call transcendental dimensions..

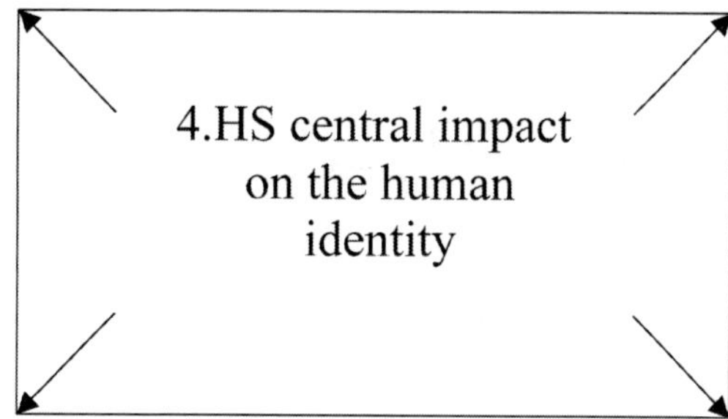

Figure 1.1.

My attempt to deepen the understanding of the profound mysterious nature of HS has led me to discover other dimensions which are hardly outlined, let alone analysed and discussed in modern social science literature: These new features of HS are expected to enrich and, thus, enhance the outlook of cultural sociology. The dimensions in question here are:

1. HS have neither weight nor volume in the material sense of the word. That is, HS do not have material nature, but they have rather non-material / transcendental/spiritual nature. Positivist social scientists are very likely to find it strange to use the terms 'weight and volume' in dealing with HS. Nonetheless, neutral objectivity strongly permits the usage of such terms and will give it a lot of meaning. It is sufficient to mention few examples to make the point on the meaning that HS do not have both volume and weight: a) Why sending letters and documents by fax and e-mail reach their destination much faster than if they were mailed by regular or even rapid mail? The explanation to this, through the concept of weightless and no volume, could be simply put this way: the process of sending letters and documents by e-mail and fax eliminates from them the factors of weight and volume. This means, that sending by fax and e-mail liberates the sent items from their material parameters (weight and volume) and as such, it returns the HS, so to speak, to their first initial natural state referred to as having neither weight nor volume.

With the absolute innate absence of weight and volume in the natural essence of the HS system, it becomes quite appropriate to understand why HS can move with high and unbelievable speed through time and space like what is assumed to be true of metaphysical and supernatural beings.

HS having no material weight and volume may help also explain how it is possible to put the enormous written material of tons of books, journals, magazines, news-papers… in few small electronic Flash Disks whose weight and volume are too little. This is possible because HS (words of the books, journals, magazines, news-papers…) having by their very nature no volume and weight need hardly material space to be contained in it. In philosophical and religious senses, HS belong to the spiritual/transcendental and non-material universe of humans. HS have their own special characteristics and laws by which they abide and ultimately make them different from the world which has both weight and volume. b) The extreme rapid speed of sound is another example which is frequently cited. The Concorde plane fast speed is often compared to that of the sound. This could be explained by the fact that the transmitted word, through the voice-sound at a short distance between individuals or at a far distance during their phone calls, has at its natural state neither weight nor volume. Consequently, the voiced-sent word is naturally predisposed to move with very rapid speed, according the HS perspective being developed, elaborated and explained here and elsewhere in this treatise.

2. Because of their non-material / transcendental nature, HS are not affected by the reduction factor when we give from them to others. For instance, when we give 50 dollars from our capital to others as charity contribution; this act reduces our capital. But the situation is quite different if we give others parts of our thought/ideas, knowledge/science or teach them our languages or spread among them our religious beliefs and cultural symbols.

3. HS have longer lifespan throughout time. Ideas, religious beliefs, cultural values and norms have long lifespan potential of survival which may last for semi-eternity. Written and spoken languages play fundamental role in the very making of HS, on the one hand, and their longer lifespan survival, on the other hand. This is because language is considered in my own perspective as the Mother of all HS. I mean by this, that HS/ culture can hardly exist without the presence of the human language in its spoken form at least. As such, one can argue that human language has a potential eternalizing mark/ seal which affects all HS and, thus, make them strongly qualified to be spiritual/ transcendental/ metaphysical: that is to say, non-material in their very deep nature. The present outlook on the long lifespan of HS helps explain the phenomena of the so called semi-eternal or eternal human thought of philosophers, scientists, scholars, religious thinkers of various civilizations since time immemorial.

Their thought potential eternity can be accounted for, first, by the use of spoken and written languages which have the eternalizing seal as just shown, and, second, by the fact that human thought belongs to the transcendental/ spiritual/metaphysical universe of HS.

4. HS can charge humans with fantastic strong energy potentials that enable them to meet and defy the great challenges in human life. In human long history, cultural values like freedom, equality, justice etc… have proven to charge human individuals, groups and larger communities with great power that defy the enormous material power of their adversary. As an example, the victory of Third World countries in the 20th century in their fight for independence from Western colonial occupation is a valid illustration of the imposing role of HS in the liberation of the colonized societies, though they were weaker militarily and materially than their Western powerful occupiers.

Modern social sciences hardly bring up what I call here transcendental/metaphysical/spiritual dimensions of HS/culture. There is still a continuing widespread silence on these very important dimensions of HS despite sociologists' increasing interest today in cultural sociology. In Thomas Kuhn's terms, current social scientists' normative paradigm still excludes the spiritual/transcendental/metaphysical features in dealing with the study of culture/HS (Alexander 2008: 157-188, Santoro 2008: 7-55). My efforts presented here in this book and elsewhere may draw some attention, among sociologists and other social scientists, to those missing features in the study of culture. But *my new HS input is unlikely to initiate a crisis in the normative paradigm* used by most sociologists today *in the study of culture*. Kuhn argues that the possibility of paradigm crisis and change can happen if the paradigm questioning is initiated and carried out by insiders of the scientific community. The present state of the perspective of cultural sociologists toward the inside transcendental nature of culture hardly promises for a coming significant change in the normative paradigm of the study of culture in the Western social sciences.

The above review of the three main stages of my independent research in the universe of HS sheds light on the new visions/insights which are quite different from those of current Western cultural sociology. As such, this treatise aspires to present in its chapters a new outlook of cultural sociology that may contest many of the premises of this branch of sociology.

LANGUAGE AND THE EMERGENCE OF HUMAN CULTURE

Based on the outlook of HS seen in this chapter, it is quite legitimate to look for the origin of the complex human culture which distinguishes the human race from the rest of the other species. The human spoken and written languages appear to be the most likely human factor behind the emergence of the phenomenon of HS/culture. It is hard to imagine the existence of the remaining elements of the HS system like religion, science, thought etc without the presence of the spoken language at least. This is why I consider *language as the Mother of all HS* in my own present perspective of analysis of the phenomenon of culture, as already mentioned. Given the central role of spoken and written languages in the birth as well as in the making of the HS system/culture as defined by anthropologists and sociologists in particular, it becomes strongly appropriate to endorse the widely cited description of philosophers and social thinkers who have seen Man as a speaking animal. As such, human language is not only the source on which depends the emergence of human culture, but it is also at the origin of the human domination over the rest of the living species through the human very sophisticated and complex cultural system. In spite of language centrality in the human identity and, consequently, in the emergence of the phenomenon of culture/HS system, the most famous anthropological definition of culture makes, nonetheless, no explicit mention of language as a central and basic elements of culture ,let alone as the major cause for human culture emergence and its making process.

The debate on the origin of culture is widely discussed today by social scientists. Though there are small differences between them, yet there is a consensus that language is the first determining factor for the emergence of human culture (Dortier: 2005-2006:26-94).

The British anthropologist Edward Bernard Taylor (1871) defined the concept of culture as follows: "Culture or civilization… is that complex whole which includes knowledge, belief, art, morals, custom, and any other capabilities and habits acquired by man as a member of society". Taylor's classical definition of culture remains implicitly silent on language while it is the constituting and the founding element/force of the phenomenon of culture itself, as I have just stated and explained. In other words, the relation between language and culture is of an organic nature. It is fair to say that Tylor's definition of culture is not fully adequate because of its negligence to clearly include language as part and founding component at the same time of the crystallization of the emergence of culture/HS system (White 1973). In view of language's extreme central role in the making of human culture, today cultural sociologists are strongly required to integrate language insightful importance in their conceptual and theoretical framework on culture. On my part, I consider language as the fourth pillar of my own perspective of cultural sociology. Thus, *the four pillars* are: 1- HS distinguish humans from the rest of the other species, 2- HS are central to the human identity, 3- HS have transcendental features and 4- Humans are privileged by spoken and written language. These basic four pillars are the fundamental parameters which make my approach to the making of cultural sociology. This book's chapters will deal with the issues raised and discussed according to the vision of that approach.

HS AND HUMAN SUPREMACY

It is clear from what has already been underlined so far in this chapter that my cultural sociological approach is, on the one hand, based on the assumptions that HS are not the bio-physiological body side of the dual human identity (HS and body) as shown in the drawing above. On the other hand, HS are the core/center of the human beings. Their supremacy on the rest of the other living beings and their domination in the world comes from the HS side in that dual human identity. In a nutshell, human supremacy and domination derive from the HS system/culture. The spoken .and written languages are the main source of the human distinction by HS system/culture. Consequently, Man is not only a speaking animal as philosophers and social thinkers have said, but *Man* is at the same time *a cultural symbolic being*. That is, the distinction of the human race from other living species by its ability to use language both in its spoken and written forms has truly made the human race qualified to be by nature the only cultural symbolic species. In the terminology of modern social sciences, it is rather legitimate to say that there is a strong correlation between the existence of the human written and the spoken languages and the emergence and the presence of the phenomenon of culture in human societies as well as of human supremacy in the world. This major importance of language in the making of human culture/HS requires that sociology and cultural sociology in particular give *greater attention to the study of language* which has been terribly missing in the literature of contemporary sociology including current cultural sociology.

CULTURAL SOCIOLOGY AS A CORE DISCIPLINE

Having established that HS are very central to human identity and are also very distinctive of the human race, HS should, consequently, be considered as *first class source/ reference* for social scientists whose studies attempt to understand and explain the behaviors of individuals as well as the societal dynamics of human societies and civilizations.

There is, therefore, a strong legitimacy for cultural sociology to be developed, expanded and defended by cultural sociologists. This branch of sociology plunges itself deeply into the basic making foundation (HS) of the identities of humans and their collectivities. Unlike other branches of sociology, which often deal with peripheral issues in the making of humans and their societies, cultural sociology addresses and focuses its prior attention on those most fundamental elements HS/culture without which neither humans nor their own communities could come into existence as we know them as distinct and leading active agents in this world. Based on this, cultural sociology ought to be strongly qualified to be seen as the essential credible knowing discipline not only in the field of sociology but in all other fields of social sciences.

DISORDER IN THE STUDY OF CULTURE

In their efforts to study culture, contemporary and modern anthropologists and sociologists have tended to study it separately from the subject (the social actor). They have focused instead on culture as a collective phenomenon in society. Various definitions of culture clearly show this. Edward B. Tylor's famous definition of culture is a good example: "Culture or civilization... is that complex whole which includes knowledge, belief, art, morals, custom and any other capabilities and habits acquired by man as member of society" (Encyclopedia of Sociology 1974: 69). So, culture is a collective phenomenon, that complex whole, and is the direct outcome of human society. Such a definition speaks of culture as the result of social context and consequently remains completely silent on the role of Man (the social actor) as a symbolic being in the making of human culture as a collective phenomenon in human societies. It could be said that anthropologists and sociologists adopted *an upside down approach* in their study of culture. They simply concluded that culture emerges from society without raising *a fundamental epistemological question* like this: could human culture, that complex whole, exist in a given context without having humans who are by nature the strongest users of symbols as it has been fully outlined so far? In other words, being innately equipped with the ability to intensely use the HS, humans become the legitimate candidates for the production of the phenomenon of culture in human societies. This treatise's chapters seek to put order in the study of culture by granting it high prior importance that social scientists should rely upon in order to comprehend and explain human single behaviors as well as collective social actions. That is, they should conceive humans in Descartes' terms:" I have HS, therefore, I am a human being".

THE HS CENTERED APPROACH

As pointed out already my own approach is different from that of the anthropologists and sociologists in the explanation of the origin of culture. While they see culture as simply the result of society, I see first that HS are central to the human agent's identity. Thus, HS determine the making of culture 'that complex whole" in human societies. Human culture is a very sophisticated collective phenomenon that can hardly be conceived without the full presence of HS as deeply inherent in the human identity. This explains the absence in animal societies of the high standard human culture. *HS make that big difference.*

As mentioned before, the French sociologist, Alain Touraine, has criticized sociologists for their negligence to focus on the social actor. He claims that sociologists are rather interested in the study of systems like the industrial and the capitalist societies. He argues as well that contemporary thought has in general minimized the subjective side of the social actor as Nietzshe, Marx and Freud had done (Wieviorka 2007 : 25-27). Touraine stresses the importance for social sciences to combine both the social system and the social actor in their analysis to understand and explain social action in society. It is neither excessive nor paradoxical to say that the idea of *society* is *a major obstacle* which bothers the development of social sciences because they are based on the separation and even the opposition between the system and the social actor, while the idea of society implies their direct link (Ibid : 28).

CULTURAL SOCIOLOGY'S URGENT NEED

Sociology's failure is twofold with regard to the study of HS/culture. On the hand, Western sociologists including the founding Fathers have not dealt with culture as a major independent and influential variable in the making of the human social action and the dynamics of human collectivities. They have rather treated culture as a dependent variable shaped mainly by social structure or/and economic imperative. On the other hand, to my knowledge, there is hardly any reference even today by cultural sociologists, let alone analysis and discussion, to the new features mentioned above in my exploration of the nature of HS. As such, I believe cultural sociology cannot progress and provide solid knowledge without focusing on the understanding of the latent/internal nature of culture/HS as I have done in my exploration of the HS universe in this book.

In other words, it is absolutely not enough for cultural sociologists to pay just more interest to culture to establish a credible cultural sociology with a 'strong program'. *The map road* to the foundation of solid cultural sociology can be achieved by cultural sociologists if they adopt in their study of culture two steps:

1. They look at culture as an independent variable and central to human identity.
2. They map profoundly (introspectively) the internal/hidden nature of culture/HS. That is, there is a strong need to go beyond the external/manifest aspects of cultural elements and get a deep knowledge of the nature of the other (hidden) sides of HS. Are not HS, like all phenomena, dualistic in their nature? Only with a good grasp of the latter could cultural sociology rightly claim, on the one hand, that it is different

from the sociology of culture and, on the one hand, and it has a real
'strong program' in the study of culture as the central basis of human
society.

THE HUNT FOR THE OTHER SIDES OF PHENOMENA

The search for the above hidden aspects of HS in my work on cultural
sociology since the 1990s may be a consequence of my previous tendency to
look for those *neglected features* in social and human phenomena. For instance, in reading predominantly Western social science books and articles in
different journals about underdevelopment in the Third World, it has struck
me that all of them have hardly referred to, let alone studied and discussed,
another dimension of underdevelopment in the societies of the South. This is
what I have called "The Other Underdevelopment/OU" (Dhaouadi 2002). I
use the OU concept to mean the psycho-cultural underdevelopment in those
countries. This type of underdevelopment can be measured in underdeveloped societies by such manifestations like the desire to imitate the West,
suffering from inferiority complex, using Western languages (English,
French…) instead of native ones, Third World heavy dependency on Western modern science and knowledge (Alatas 2003: 599-613, Alatas 1974: 691-
9, Alatas Syed 2000: 23-45) the diffusion of Western cultural values in the
developing societies of the South.

In response to this academic and intellectual silence on the OU, I have set
out to explore this forgotten underdevelopment especially in the Third
World.

Likewise, my intense exploration into the HS territory, in this treatise and
elsewhere, has led me to discover other hidden dimensions in them. As
mentioned earlier; I asked for example, why humans grow and mature very
slowly on the body level compared with the rapid body growth and maturation among the other species and why humans have longer lifespan than
many other living beings?

As stressed before, my search to answer these questions has made me
discover that HS play a crucial role in both the human slow body growth and
maturation and, consequently, in the human longer lifespan. This hidden link
is hardly explicitly mentioned both in natural and social sciences. In Randall
Collins' terms, this may be seen as a sociological insight of a new type of
what he calls Non-Obvious Sociology (Collins 1992). It may be claimed that
hidden/non-obvious aspects of phenomena can be more important for their
understanding and explanation: " non-obvious sociology pulls some insights
out of the treasure chest, letting us see the underlying conditions that are
moving us"(Collins 1992:188).

The hidden link between cultural/HS and the biological in the human entity is an obvious example of my *interdisciplinary approach* in this book. It has to do with the interaction between the two poles (body and HS) of the human identity. That is, the slow body growth and maturation of humans are implicitly affected by their interaction with the *HS* which are considered in this work as *the crucial determining factor* that shapes and influences so many aspects of the human identity and its various individual and collective behaviors. This vision of HS can only enhance and promote cultural sociology's good standing among today social sciences.

REFERENCES

Alatas, F. (2003). Academic Dependency and the Global Division of Labor in the Social sciences. *Current Sociology*, *51*(6), 599-613.

Alatas, S. (1974). The Captive Mind in Development Studies. *International Social Science Journal*, *34*(1), 9-25.

Alatas, S. (2000). Intellectual Imperialism: Definitions, Traits, and Problems. *Southeast Asian Journal of Social Science*, *28*(1), 23-45.

Bonnell, V.E., Hunt, L. (Eds). (1999). *Beyond The Cultural Turn*. Berkeley: University of California Press.

Collins, R. (1992). *Sociological Insight: An Introduction to Non-Obvious Sociology*. New York: Oxford University Press.

Crane, D. (ed.).1995. *The Sociology of Culture*. Oxford (UK): Blackwell.

Daloz, J-P, Semashko, L.M, Erdemir, A. (2003). [Review of the book *The Meanings of Social Life: A Cultural Sociology*, by Jeffrey C. Alexander.] *International Sociology Review of Books* (ISRB), *21*(6).

Dhaouadi, M. (2002). *Globalization of the Other Underdevelopment: Third World Cultural Identities*. Kuala Lumpur: A.S. Noordeen.

Encyclopedia of Sociology. (1974). Guilford, Dushkin, Publishing Group, Inc.

Hoover, K. (1988). *The Elements of Social Scientific Thinking*. New York: St. Martin's Press.

Spillman, L. (Ed.). (2007). *Cultural Sociology*. Oxford (UK): Blackwell Publishing.

Wieviork, M. (Ed.) (2007). *Les sciences sociales en mutation*. Auxerre Cedex: Editions Sciences Humaines.

NOTE

I use in this book the terms "Human Symbols" (HS) instead of "Cultural Symbols"(CS) which I have used before; because the use of HS eliminates the vagueness which may be found in the word 'cultural' which is being used recently in the human and social science study of animals. Consequently, for better transparency I choose the word 'human' instead of 'cultural' to mean simply by that all those symbols which distinguish the human species from the rest of the living species. These symbols/HS are: spoken and written language, thought, knowledge/science, religion, myths, laws, cultural values and norms.

New Intellectual Concepts for Cultural Sociology

INTRODUCTION

Following the setting in the previous chapter, I would like to outline here a number of *my linked concepts* and features to HS that have appeared in my own work over the past fifteen years or so. The concepts and features in question involve the following: the notion of the Other Underdevelopment (OU) meaning the forgotten linguistic-cultural and psychological underdevelopment in the Arab and Third World, Tunisian woman Franco-Arabe and Parisian accent and Conspiratory bilinguism in North African societies.

In my field research on Tunisian society, I chose examples in which the social actors were found to be great users of HS, and particularly language, the Mother of all HS. This chapter concentrates on the widespread use of code-switching and Adaa (curse words), prevalent among Tunisian women. This falls well within the above concept of the Other Underdevelopment (OU).

THE CONCEPT OF THE OTHER UNDERDEVELOPMENT

In 1983, I published my first article in Arabic about what I called *the Other Underdevelopment* in the Maghreb (Dhaouadi, 1983: 20-41). The Other Underdevelopment (OU) is the oral and written *under-use of the national language* (Arabic) in Algeria, Tunisia and Morocco, as the result of the linguistic impact of French colonisation on these developing societies (Dhaouadi, 1988: 219-234). I see the OU as a form of underdevelopment that strikes at language and HS of those societies. It could be considered as the

most dangerous kind of underdevelopment that affects human societies, because it threatens their language(s)and HS, the very core and most precious
and fundamental HS heritage of their entire existence, as spelled out in the
precedent chapter.

In spite of this, the OU is hardly dealt with, in either the West or the East,
in the current social science literature on development/underdevelopment,
which is, in itself, a sign of *academic dependency* in the non-Western world
(Alatas, 2003: 599-613, 2006). Modern social sciences have rather focused
instead on the economic side of underdevelopment in the Third World and, in
so doing, has violated the ethics of scientific objectivity. Social scientists
have underemphasized the non-economic dimensions of underdevelopment
in New Nations. In other words, they have neglected many features of underdevelopment, because they obviously have not looked at Third World underdevelopment as a complex phenomenon that comprises *many kinds of under-
developments*, of which the OU is just one. Furthermore, the silence of social
scientists on the issue of the OU both as an empirical fact in many Third
World societies clearly undermines the credibility of their research on underdevelopment[1] .

LINGUISTIC ISSUES UNDER SCRUTINY

A special subfeature of the OU can be found, especially, among Tunisian
women who have more than primary school level of education. These wom-
en tend to be more involved in code-switching than their Tunisian male
counterparts, since they use more French words in their Tunisian Arabic
dialect "the Franco-Arabe" (Dhaouadi, 1982: 124-137, 2003: 417-435, 1986:
46-66, 1996a: 81-91). They also practice a more pronounced Parisian accent
than Tunisian men when they speak and read French (Dhaouadi, 1996b: 107-
125; 2002c: 41-53). Seen from the perspective of HS, *these Tunisian women
are*, therefore, *bigger users of French cultural-linguistic symbols*.

Thus, these Tunisian women's use of French words and expressions, in
their Tunisian Arabic dialects, has two characteristics: 1. they use more
French words and expressions than their male counterparts and, 2. they have
a more pronounced Parisian accent. From a methodological point of view, it
is legitimate here, to differentiate between *two types* of Franco-Arabe prevalent in Tunisian society: one masculine and one used by females. The socio-
psychological causes of this cultural-linguistic symbolism need to be fully
described and analysed.

THE SOCIAL PSYCHOLOGICAL DIMENSIONS OF THE FEMALE FRANCO-ARABE

The mixing of Arabic and French (the Franco-Arabe), prevalent among the Tunisian population, has its roots in the French colonization of Tunisia from 1881 to 1956. The theory of imitation developed by Ibn Khaldun, the Arab Muslim historian and sociologist of the Middle Ages (1332-1406), may explain why the encounter between the French colonizer and the colonized Tunisians led, on one hand, to the emergence of the Franco-Arabe in Tunisia and, on the other, to the almost total absence of what we might call an Arabo-Frenco among the French colonizers. According to Ibn Khaldun, "the vanquished always seek to imitate the victor's distinctive characteristics including his dress, occupation and other particularities and customs." (Ibn Khaldun, 1969: 116) However, while the Franco-Arabe is a general socio-psycho-linguistic fact in contemporary Tunisia, males and females do not utilize it in the same way.

Interviews as well as direct and group observation have clearly shown that literary and educated Tunisian women have decisively a more pronounced inclination towards adopting more French in their spoken Arabic.[2] In Khaldunian terms, we could very well ask the question now, what lies behind this greater level of imitation by these Tunisian women of the French language as *a cultural-linguistic symbol*. In other words, what are the socio-psychological factors that make them more prone to use French more frequently in their Arabic conversation? What is at stake here is the identification of certain specific factor(s) that might account for this greater inclination to use the Franco-Arabe among Tunisian literary and educated women..My present research in the field has enabled me to identify *two major forces* that might explain the female Franco-Arabe in Tunisia. They are both of a socio-psychological nature, caused by what might be called *the symptom of dual self contempt* (Dhaouadi, 1986: 46-66). On the one hand, there is an inferiority complex vis-à-vis the French, (or the West, in general) shared by both males and females in today's Tunisian society (Memmi, 1957). On the other, literary and educated Tunisian women suffer from another inferiority complex typical of a largely male-dominated society. The mentality, traditions and social structure of Tunisian society had and still obstruct, in certain cases, women's easy access and full participation in major aspects of modern life. In functional terms, the literary and educated Tunisian women's frequent resort to Franco-Arabe (as a cultural-linguistic symbol) basically serves a *psychological function*. It is a symbolic compensatory solution, which gives them the impression that they are bridging the equality gap between them and their male counterparts. The use of French as a cultural symbolic weapon serves two purposes as far as these Tunisian women are concerned: It lifts them up in a manner that makes them feel, consciously or unconsciously, closer to the image and status of the former colonizer, i.e., the French who embodies for them a high image of self-esteem. The intention behind imitating the French linguistically is, therefore, to reduce the burden of the inferiority complex still felt by Tunisian men and women vis-à-vis the perceived dominant Westerners. Tunisian women's frequent use of French appears, therefore, to be a symbolic gesture through which *they peacefully protests* against the social order in their society, a social order that still sets obstacles which block their easy access to certain aspects of modern life enjoyed by their male counterparts.

In addition, the pursuit of modernity in Tunisian society increases socio-psychological pressure and stress on women, and raises their anxiety level (Hays, 1987). In socio-psychological terms, the female use of Franco-Arabe could be seen as the outcome of two types of stressful practices, which the literary and educated Tunisian women are especially the victims. These are: 1. the sense of degradation feeling, which is an outcome of the relationship between the dominant former colonizer and the dominated colonized Tunisians and, 2. the relative oppressiveness of the prevailing traditions, mentality and social structure in Tunisian society. This is felt more by the literary and educated female population who aspires for greater modernity (Hays, 1987). It is clear that the inferiority complex plaguing these Tunisian women is the outcome of both social and psychological forces and, as such, their socio-psychological state is more likely to be more vulnerable to social contradictions and psychological tensions (Hays, 1987). There is hardly a need to point out how *the three theoretical concepts* outlined above can help explain the linguistic behavior patterns of literary and educated Tunisian women.

THE SOCIAL PSYCHOLOGICAL DIMENSIONS OF ADÀA

Adàa is an Arabic word which means the oral use of Arabic words and sentences to inflict harm on and wish bad luck for someone. It is a form of "cursing" and is more widespread among women in Tunisian society. It is fair to state that this widely used female form of Tunisian discourse has nothing to do with female biology. Had it been so, it would have been a common past, present and future feature among the female population of the world, regardless of their socio-cultural differences.

Adàa hardly exists, for instance, in both American and Canadian societies. Thus, it becomes a legitimate domain of sociological research. As mentioned above, the sociologist can easily say that Adàa, in Tunisian society, is a female linguistic phenomenon widespread predominantly among women. Its roots are first and foremost of a social nature. This is not a recent phenomenon in Tunisian society; it has been part of *a cultural-symbolic heritage* prevalent among Tunisian women in general.

THE SOCIAL HISTORY OF ADÀA IN THE ARAB WORLD

Social researchers must shed light on the history of those social forces that helped bring about the widespread phenomenon of Adàa among Tunisian women. The Arab sociologist, Zuheir Hatab, is perhaps the only known Arab author to have made implicit reference to some of the socio-historical causes that could help explain and account for the emergence of Adàa in Arab societies at large (Hatab, 1980). Although the determination of the precise date of the emergence of Adàa would help come closer to a better understanding of the phenomenon, I nonetheless focus my attention in this chapter on the diagnosis of its socio-psychological dimensions, based on what the phenomenon itself implies. An appropriate reading and interpretation may convey an adequate image of both the state of society as well as of the social status of women in it.

Adàa is more likely to surface, and even take root, in societies where the following *cultural-symbolic characteristics* are common features: alphabetical and intellectual illiteracy, prevalence of superstition and strong beliefs in invisible and mysterious forces like the devil, demons (Jinn), Saints, magicians, etc…

Like other linguistic discourses, Adàa unveils certain aspects of society's inner workings. It is a sort of mirror that reflects, in a cultural-symbolic manner, the social condition of individuals and groups in a given period of a society's history. In short, Adàa is one of the telling indicators of a society's grave cultural-symbolic backwardness. It should be added to the list of factors that indicate underdevelopment as spelled out in the literature relevant to modern sociological studies on underdevelopment in the Third World in particular. *Adàa* may be viewed as a clear *component of the Other Underdevelopment* which erodes and undermines both the psychological and cultural-symbolic dimensions of the individual's personality, as described earlier.

NEW INTELLECTUAL CONCEPTS FOR CULTURAL SOCIOLOGY

According to Zuheir Hatab, Arab families and the societies in which they lived witnessed a grave decline in thought and behaviour, especially in the sixteenth and the seventeenth centuries. This means that Adàa has had recorded, in a cultural-symbolic manner, the deterioration of Arab societies in general, of which Tunisian society is a sub-system.

ADÀA AND ITS SOCIAL PSYCHOLOGICAL MEANING FOR TUNISIAN WOMEN

I have considered above some of the socio-cultural-symbolic meanings that could be inferred from Adàa, regarding the state of Arab societies in a given historical period. However, the most important question relevant to the core of this chapter is the following: what are the precise socio-psychological dimensions of Adàa as far as Tunisian women are concerned? As indicated above, Adàa is predominantly an oral discourse prevalent among women in Tunisian society. According to Zuheir Hatab's perspective, it could be explained by the overall deterioration in the social status of Arab women, during the decadent periods of Arab history. "Because of her widespread illiteracy, lack of societal experience and isolation, the Arab woman becomes the one member of the family, and society, most predisposed to react favorably to superstitious beliefs and ideas (cultural symbols), and most inclined to take them at face value and as basis for her behavior and actions (Hatab, 1980: 175).

In sociological terms, *the phenomenon of Adàa* among the Arab (Tunisian) female population is *the outcome of stubborn socio-cultural-symbolic determinism.*

On the psychological level, the discourse of Adàa among Tunisian women unambiguously hints at the fact that they were, at given times at least, incapable of dealing directly and personally with many issues and events that have affected, preoccupied and challenged them. Feeling helpless, weak and in a state of defeat, they seek help and intervention from others. What aggravates their situation is the fact that Adàa is a way of calling upon invisible and metaphysical beings to intervene, take-over and pring order in their lives. In acting this way, they are only exacerbating their psychological state of powerlessness. The intermediary beings to which they appeal for help belong neither to the real material worlds nor to their own daily life. By resorting to Adàa, they are ultimately seeking the help of an imaginary and illusory universe that could hardly help bring about real and substantive change to their socio-psychological situation.

THE CONDITION OF TUNISIAN WOMEN AND THE PARISIAN ACCENT

Two important psychological and social reasons continue to predispose Tunisian women, more than men to adopt a Parisian accent when speaking or reading French and explain also the tendency among them to intersperse the Tunisian Arabic dialect with French words and expressions (the Franco-Arabe). In other words, both the Parisian accent and the greater use of French in the Tunisian Arabic dialect, when perceived as linguistic symbols, could be interpreted as signs of the contemporary Tunisian women's *degraded social status and their troubled psychological state.* Their socio-psychological situation makes them both keener than Tunisian men to imitate the linguistic-cultural symbols of the former French colonizer, and more eager than men to reach out for *the cultural symbols of modernity.* Both of these behavioral patterns could be seen as signs of what is called in modern psychology as the 'status frustration's syndrome.

THE PECKING ORDER AMONG THE THREE SOCIAL ACTORS

In order to involve the sociological perspective in my analysis, let us look at the phenomenon from the perspective of the social theory of imitation.

The act of imitation implies at least the presence of and interaction between two parties: the imitator and the imitated. During the French colonization of Tunisia, there were three parties involved: Tunisian women, Tunisian men and the French colonizers. Interaction between these three parties took place according to the so-called pecking order: according to the hierarchical structure that dominated the relationship between these three social actors. On the one hand, during the French colonial period (1881-1956), the French occupiers were the dominators and Tunisian men and women were the dominated. On the other, Tunisian society was male oriented, resulting in stark inequality between the sexes. In this triad setting, Tunisian women were subject to *two types of domination* and, consequently, were the most powerless of the three.[3]

a-The continuing pecking order

With Tunisia's independence in 1956, the situation underwent significant change for the parties concerned. Though the French occupation of Tunisia ended and soon after, most of the French inhabitants left the country, the shadow of French domination did not fade from the imagination of the independent people of Tunisia. France is still present among the Tunisians, through its cultural symbols, especially its language, culture and thought, and the Tunisians' somewhat semi-colonized mind still sees and feels its presence. As a well developed society, France is still highly visible in developing Tunisia, through tourism, the written media and the lively transmitted images on French and European television stations, seen regularly by Tunisian viewers. After independence, the dominant/dominated relationship between the French and the Tunisians took the form of a relationship between the developed and the developing. In other words, Tunisians continue to suffer from the syndrome of inequality in their relationship with the French, their former colonizers.

b-Persistent inequality between the sexes

The Tunisian social scene witnessed considerable positive change in the social status of women. Today, all girls can go to school, women have joined in full swing the job market and several progressive laws in the field of gender equality, have been enacted. Tunisian women are today the avant-garde of the Arab world as far as women's rights are concerned. Yet, total equality between men and women, in all aspects of life, is yet to become a reality in independent modern Tunisia. It is true that this state of affairs is far from being peculiar to Tunisia. Inequality between the sexes still exists even in the most advanced Western societies. In other words, in terms of equality, Tunisian women still lag behind their male counterparts on few fronts, while considerable gains have greatly enhanced their social status in the last five decades or so. They are still more at a disadvantage than Tunisian men, especially regarding what may be called 'modernity's benefits.[4] The net result is a continuing, though much weakened, hierarchical order among the former French colonizers, Tunisian men and Tunisian women. This pecking order is quite thin though. There has been some change, since Tunisia's independence in favour of more equality in the relationship between independent Tunisians and the former French colonisers, and locally, between the sexes. In this hierarchal triad, however, the position of Tunisian women tends to stay in third place. This is likely to continue to predispose women to wish to use French cultural symbols, such as Franco-Arabe and the Parisian accent in order *to compensate* for their third class status within the triad social order.

WHO IMITATES WHOM AND HOW?

The modern social science theory of imitation suggests that the weaker party is more inclined to imitate the stronger one. This is in line with Ibn Khaldun's law of imitation. As we have seen before, Tunisian women suffer from a dual domination. The traditional male dominated society continues, in certain cases, to block their social mobility, restrict their access to the wider benefits of modernity and limit their free development and self-fulfilment. Thus, Tunisian women in particular are more compelled to look for an outlet that allows them to liberate themselves to a certain degree from the burden of the double domination they face. Their inclination toward imitating cultural-symbolically the dominant French appears to be the result of at least *three reasons*:

1. The French were once physically and now cultural-symbolically the dominant party in the triad order referred to earlier, and are, thus, more likely to be imitated by the most dominated party (Tunisian women).

2. Tunisian women's cultural-symbolic imitation of the French liberates them, somehow, psychologically and, to a certain extent socially, from some of the strict traditional cultural features of the significantly male-dominated society.
3. By imitating the French (Western) dominant party, Tunisian women are attempting to minimize the stress caused by their desire for modernity in a society that continues to exercise, in certain cases, a double standard regarding gender equality (Hays, 1987).

In other words, the assumption that Tunisian women are more deprived of modernity's benefits than Tunisian men compels them to seek *peaceful cultural-symbolic means* to express their frustration. They opt, so to speak, for a non-violent way to protest against their male dominated society. Furthermore, their imitation of the French (Westerners) is hardly limited to their adoption of a Parisian accent when they speak or read French. As pointed out earlier, they are also known to be more prone than men to mix French words with their Arabic dialect (Franco-Arabe) in everyday conversations (Dhaouadi, 1986: 46-66). Tunisian women also appear to be more involved in birthday celebrations than Tunisian men, as evidenced by the organisation of birthday parties for their children, a habit that has become relatively widespread since independence among a significant majority of Tunisian mothers not only in big cities but also in towns and villages. The adoption of the Parisian accent, the tendency to use more French words and/or expressions in their Arabic conversation and the widespread birthday celebrations converge to indicate that Tunisian women are more in need of imitating modern French (Western) cultural symbols. To speak French with a Parisian accent means to be somewhat as modern as the Parisian themselves, the most modern among all the modern French people. Behind the Parisian accent and use of the French language in general, there is more than what the ear can hear. The persistent use of the Parisian accent by today's Tunisian women culturally symbolizes becoming modern like the Parisians. In sociological terms, the feeling of being obstructed by the traditional structure of a male dominated society compels modern Tunisian women to reach out for certain cultural symbols of modernity that do not upset Tunisian men. The Parisian accent, the greater use of French words and expressions, and birthday celebrations appear to satisfy on two accounts. On the one hand, the Tunisian woman's self-esteem and desire to become modern seem to be easily and adequately fulfilled by the use of those cultural symbols. On the other, the Tunisian male population apparently does not mind that Tunisian women can have access to modernity by using linguistic-cultural symbols tolerated by the rules of a male dominated society.

Thus, the belief that Tunisian women are more prone to get cultural-symbolically involved in a wide range of French (Western) imitative behavioural patterns is more than just a single limited act. As described, it covers a number of linguistic-cultural-symbolic acts (the Parisian accent, more use of French words and expressions with Arabic and birthday celebrations) which ultimately make up an entire coherent cultural symbolic system. All these different acts reveal, unequivocally, Tunisian women's pressing desire for for many aspects of Western modernity of which they are deprived of in their male dominated society[5] . Their main aim is to have greater access to the cultural-symbolic system of modernity they are reaching for and upon which they are concentrating their cultural symbolic imitative efforts. Cultural-symbolically, it is a compensation for the missing benefits of modernity. Their greater deprivation (compared with their Tunisian male counterparts) from the advantages of modernity gains makes them most eligible candidates for a full-fledged cultural linguistic imitation of modern French/Western people in general. In other words, this is likely a symptom that they suffer more from *the Other Underdevelopment* than their male counterparts.

Thus, the continuous overwhelming use of the Parisian accent by the majority of today's Tunisian women, when speaking or reading in French, should be understood in light of what has been already underlined, namely that the historical argument that accounts for the contemporary Tunisian women's Parisian accent is far from adequate. Without analyzing the social situation and the psychological state of contemporary Tunisian women, as well as their use of cultural symbols in response to those conditions, no lucid understanding or explanation of the origin as well as the ongoing use of the Parisian accent, can be secured. The question of the Parisian accent is hardly a matter of plain history, as Professor Skiks (1992) claims. Such a view excludes the impact of society's on-going dynamics on the use of language (the Mother of all HS) through time and space. An accent in any given language is always potentially subject to change by the people who use it. When it persists, as is the case with the Parisian accent among contemporary Tunisian women, we must look for a structural and functional perspective that offers a credible explanation. Such explanation is that the continuous use of the Parisian accent by the majority of Tunisian women will continue to fulfil socio-psychological needs as long as the Tunisian women remain the most disadvantaged party in certain areas of the pecking order of modern Tunisian society.

CONSPIRATORY TUNISIAN BILINGUALISM

I finish this chapter by the presentation of my newest concept (2010) which is related to the other previous concepts presented above. It has to do with what I call *Conspiratory bilingualism* as explained in the following: the Tunisian society uses two languages: Arabic as its national language and

French as a colonial language. The written and oral presence of Arabic and French in Tunisia creates *two types of bilingualism*: A- a bilingualism which does not blame the use of French among Tunisians. This bilingualism is the most widespread in Tunisia today. B- a bilingualism that blames the use of French between Tunisians. This is represented by a very tiny minority of Tunisians. These two bilingualisms are also associated with *two forms of Arabization*. The first common meaning of the term Arabization is the promotion of the wide societal use of Arabic instead of French in various sectors of Tunisian society. The second meaning of Arabization is what I refer to as *psychological Arabization*. The latter means the establishment by Tunisians of a normal close relationship with Arabic, their national language.

My research shows that there is rather a negative relationship between type A of bilingualism and the first and the second type of Arabization. Bilingualism A does not strongly promote either of the two patterns of Arabization. In contrast, bilingualism B is very committed to the full promotion of the two Arabizations in Tunisia. The social psychological analysis of the Tunisian linguistic scene shows that bilingualism A is a *Conspiratory type of bilingualism*. Its continuing prominence in today Tunisia is the outcome of four main factors: 1- the spread of French in the Tunisian society during the French colonization (1881-1956). 2- throughout that period, many Tunisians went to schools in Tunisia where French language and its culture were dominant and furthermore some of them attended later French universities in France. 3-The graduates of these schools and universities have taken over the major responsibilities (Presidents of the country, Prime ministers, ministers, governors...) to rule and administer the country after independence. 4- In Pierre Bourdieu's terms, those French educated Tunisians have *re-produced themselves linguistically* in governing the Tunisian society by giving great importance to the presence and use of French and its culture in independent Tunisia. Consequently, the attitude today of a majority of Tunisians toward Arabic, their national language, can legitimately be described as *conspiratory* or *non-national* .

REFERENCES

Alatas, F. (2003). Academic Dependency and the Global Division of Labour in the Social Science. *Current Sociology, 51*(6), 599-613.

Dhaouadi, M. (2006). *Culture Between Islamic and Social Science Perspectives* (in Arabic). Beirut: Dar al Kitab al Jadid Ltd.

Dhaouadi, M. (2003). Tunisian Women's Strained Social Status as Reflected in the Verbal Discourses of Adàa and the Franco-Arabe. *Revue d'histoire maghrébine, 30*(112).

Dhaouadi, M. (2002a). *Globalization of the Other Underdevelopment: Third World Cultural Identities*. Kuala Lumpur: A. S. Noordeen.

Dhaouadi, M. (2002b). *The Other Underdevelopment: The Globalization of the Cultural Identities Crisis in the Arab World and the Third World* (in Arabic). Tunis: Al Atlasiyyah Publisher.

Dhaouadi, M. (2002c). A Socio-Psychological Theoretical Analysis of the French Parisian Accent Use Among Tunisian Females and Males. *Journal of King Saud University, 14*(2).

Dhaouadi, M. (1996a). The Feminine Franco-Arabe in the Maghreb. *Dirāsāt ʿArabiyyah* (in Arabic), *32*(3-4).

Dhaouadi, M. (1996 b). Un essai de théorisation sur le penchant vers l'accent parisien chez la femme tunisienne. *International Journal of the Sociology of Language, 122.*

Dhaouadi, M. (1986). Code-Switching as a Linguistic Behavior of Dominated Maghrebians (in Arabic). *Arab Journal for the Humanities, 6*(*22*).

Dhaouadi, M. (1983). The Other Underdevelopment in the Maghreb (in Arabic). *Al Mustaqbal Al ʿArabī, 47, 20-41.*

Dhaouadi, M. (1982a). Les Racines du franco-arabe féminin au Maghreb. *Arab Journal of Language Studies, 2*(2).

Dhaouadi, M. (1982b). The Roots of the Maghrebian Franco-Arabe. *Shuʾūn ʿArabiyyah* (in Arabic), *22.*

Dhaouadi, M. (1974). Our Franco-Arabe. *Al Fikr Magazine* (in Arabic). Tunis.

Dortier, J-F. (2004). *Dictionnaire des sciences humaines.* Auxerre Cedex.

Hatab, Z. (1980). *The Evolution of the Structures of the Arab Family* (in Arabic). Beirut: Institute of Arab Development.

Hays, P. (1987). *Modernization, Stress and Psychopathology in Tunisian Women* (Ph.D. Thesis, University of Hawaï).-Ibn Khaldun (1969). *The Muqaddimah: An Introduction to History.* Translated from the Arabic by Franz Rosenthal; abridged and edited by N. J. Dawood. Princeton, NJ: Princeton University Press.

Memmi, A. (1957). *Portrait du colonisé précédé du portrait du colonisateur.* Paris: Gallimard.

NOTES

1. My notion of the Other Underdevelopment/OU is the result of genuine criticism, which I address in particular to the modern sociology of development/underdevelopment.

2. For instance, an overwhelming majority of Tunisians when asked who mixes more Arabic with French, men or women, chose women as the greater users of French. This repeated common sense impression can hardly be dismissed as unfounded, especially when further supported by meticulous social science research techniques like the ones referred to in this chapter. Modern social science literature on the relationship between gender and language use is still poor despite its steady growth in recent years. Peter Trudill, for instance, advances a similar argument to the one advanced in this study, namely that specific language use reflect the social and psychological situation of its user. He says that, "Men in our society can be rated socially by their occupation, their earning power and perhaps by their other abilities, in other words, by what they do. For the most part, however, this is not possible for women. It may be, therefore, that they are instead to be rated on how they appear. Since they are not rated by their occupation or by their occupational success, other signals of state, including speech, are correspondingly more important" (*Language in Society*: Sex, Covert Prestige and Linguistic Change in the Urban British English of Norwich; vol. 1, no. 2, Oct. 1972. pp. 179-194).

3. The double standard ethics between the two sexes is still strong in certain sectors of today's Tunisian society. The cultural value system of the latter still exercises more constraints on the female population toward things associated with modernity. Three empirical examples from the Tunisian social scene are sufficient to make the point: (a) women's mobility after sunset in greatly restricted. They hardly can attend theatrical plays, movies, shows, intellectual events, etc, at night, if they are not accompanied by male companions, in particular. (b) Tunisian cultural norms still do not permit Tunisian women to smoke in public. And (c) Going to cafés to have a coffee, or eat a cake… is still strongly a male activity in Tunisian society.

4. Modernity's benefits basically refer to three things: 1) more equality between the sexes in their social order; 2) more freedom of movement for women in society; 3) more freedom of expression for women in public.

5. Smoking in public, a sign of modernity and liberation for some Tunisian females, is still seen as unacceptable behaviour by Tunisian society.

Chapter Three

Social Sciences Need for HS Paradigm

THE CONCEPT OF THE HUMAN SYMBOLIC SOUL (HSS)

As pointed out before, HS are seen in this chapter as being intrinsically imbued with transcendental/metaphysical qualities whose impact and role in shaping human behaviors of individuals, groups, and the dynamics of societies are viewed as crucial.[1] The centrality of HS both in the making of the most human distinct identity and its social action justifies the priority which must be given to their analysis and comprehension. This epistemological outlook on the nature of HS should be the privileged frame of analysis for the social scientist who aspires to establish more credible intellectual paradigms, which could help disclose the nature of the latent yet powerful moving forces of HS which trigger the behaviors of individuals and the dynamics of societies.

In other words, the HS that the human species possesses must be the *main source* that psychologists, sociologists, anthropologists and political scientists ought to consult and refer to in any ambitious scientific endeavor which seriously aims at improving the levels of understanding and explaining the behavior of the individuals as well as that of human collectivities. In short, being central to the very identity-making as well as to the behavior of social actors in any society and any culture, HS could legitimately be called *the Human Symbolic Soul* of human social actors.[2]

Giving HS a prominent role in the study of the social actor's behaviors and society's dynamics restores *the essential humanistic touch* to the mainstream work of behavioral social sciences. That humanistic dimension has been considerably lost under the impact of both Behaviorism and Structuro-Functionalism. The former often studies human behavior according to S-R contingency or the rules that govern animal behavior. Modern Structuro-

Functionalism, on its part, examines social action as shaped and determined by no more than the constraining social facts (faits sociaux) and the social structures.

SOCIAL SCIENCES NEED FOR HS PARADIGM

The major thesis to be developed throughout the pages of this chapter aims essentially to accomplish *two goals:* to establish a theoretical framework on the nature and the role of HS as key forces to the determination of single or collective human behavior. Viewed in this way, the insights of HS are expected to enhance the social scientist's scientific credibility. In other words, I aspire to make a social science contribution to Basic Research in the field of HS, and try to apply my theoretical perspective in an empirical manner on a sample of behaviors drawn from different societies, cultures, and civilizations.

The full and conclusive success in combining the theoretical and the applied levels in the behavioral social sciences remains, however, *an ideal.* The measure of one's theory's highest credibility is nothing more than coming closer to the realization of a genuine synthesis between the applied and the theoretical in the world of the behavioral social sciences.

OUR EVER SMALLER WORLD

Alvin Toffler, the well-known American thinker, has stated that humankind has gone through *two major revolutions*: the Agricultural and Industrial Revolutions. Today, humanity embarks on its third and most important revolution. It is *the Third Wave* in which the Communication/ Information Revolution is a prominent feature (Toffter 1980) The latter is especially displayed in the formidable capacity that humans increasingly have in dealing with *HS*: word, thought, belief, science, cultural norms and values, voice, image, etc. The modern techniques, in Ellul's terminology, of printing and sending voice and image have reached a high degree of efficiency and precision in diffusing HS from one place to another with stunning speed. This breakthrough in the field of communication has made the world renowned Canadian communication expert, Marshal McLuhan, state that our vast world of different civilizations, people and tribes scattered here and there around the globe has become a small village whose quarters are practically separated by no frontiers (McLuhan 1967).

The continuing advancement in the high quality technology of information and communication since McLuhan's famous statement ought to oblige us to modify that statement to update it—though surely for a short time—to the new communication/information reality that the earth's population experiences today. It could be said at this moment of humanity's history that the entire vast planet earth is no more than a small room. This may suggest that the universe of HS appears to be of a different nature that does not pertain, to the physico-materialistic world. The successive milestones that information/ communication technology has reached and continues to reach, in the domain of the diffusion of HS, defy the very basis of the traditional logic of the human five senses.

Today, any individual on this earth or in space could practically hear the voice of any event and watch its image(s) in color at the very moment of its happening. This is regardless of the formidable distances that could separate that individual from the scene where the event is taking place. It is now a common practice all over the world that newspapers and magazines publish their issues of the same content simultaneously in different cities of the same country or in cities in various continents. Likewise, it has become possible for any person to send printed letters, documents, etc., by fax, by Internet and Cell phone to any individual, institution, or association around the globe. The addressee receives the faxed or the emailed material in a matter of minutes or seconds. This is because HS have neither weight nor volume, as explained in chapter I.

HS TRANSCENDENTALITY

Because of the absence of volume and weight in HS, I claim in this book that the universe of HS is impregnated with transcendental/ spiritual/metaphysical dimensions as elaborated earlier. Without this new insight on HS, instant communication with the other person(s) through the spoken or the written word and through the image in spite of the obstacles of mountains, seas, deserts and oceans would be an event that could only belong to the world of the impossible or that of pure human imagination.

This type of happening is hardly acceptable by traditional material human logic. From a common sense point of view, this kind of happening is usually confined to the will of supernatural beings like the gods and the spirits. Today's unbelievably speedy communication through the manipulation of HS can only endorse Toffler's statement that considers the third revolution (the Third Wave) as the most important one among the three great revolutions that humanity has experienced so far. There is scarcely any doubt that it is the greatest revolution as far as the instant diffusion of HS on a worldwide scale.

This newly acquired human potential (the third revolution) has indeed liberated humans most from the physico-materialistic constraints and has, thus, made them act with a greater freedom. This has enabled them to possess a new power which has come to resemble rather the metaphysical power in the sense that it could do whatever it desires through time and space. What is interesting to underline here is that people of almost all social categories and classes have been primarily deeply astonished by the modern information/ communication technology and, as such, they have paid little attention, if any, to the role that *the intrinsic transcendental nature of HS* could play in the materialization of Toffler's Third Wave.

Communication and information experts remain generally *silent* on what I have called the transcendental/spiritual/ metaphysical dimensions of HS (McLuhan 1967). Though rigid Positivism is increasingly under attack in the behavioral social sciences, communication and information specialists have hardly been able to speak aloud about the no weight no volume (transcendental/ spiritual/metaphysical) characteristics of HS (Brody 1970) as explained especially in chapter I of this work.

The intangible/non-sensory qualities of the universe of HS are remarkably manifest when we compare them with other components that are parts of the human entity. For instance, the human body and its smell are clearly part of that entity, so are the human voice and the spoken and written words. As outlined, the modern communication techniques have scored a high mark in becoming able to send off instantly the spoken/written word, the voice and the image from any place on the planet earth or in vast space to any other desired destination in both of them. With those communication break-throughs, whose high level of quality steadily continues to improve, we can say with considerable objectivity that we are sort of entering *the world of wondrous things and miracles.* While our body floats in space or walks on earth, its lively image can be at once moved anywhere on earth or in space. Likewise, while the most advanced communication technology remains powerless as far as the transmission of our body's smell, so it could be smelled at fairly short distances, the earlier simple communication technology of radio and telephone was able to transmit the spoken word and the human voice to great distances around the globe.

The ever-increasing smallness of our world should not be solely attributed to the mere improvement of modern transmission/ communication techniques. The transcendental nature of the HS, already outlined, should be taken into account as well. In other words, the order of HS is different from the materialistic/sensory order of things. It has its own laws and characteristics that resemble, to an extent, those of the supernatural world. This is a plain epistemological statement on the nature of HS. Like empirical field work, epistemological questions are often needed to be raised part of as a research methodology that helps the social scientist, or any scientist for that matter, improve his/her understanding of the phenomenon in question.

My emphasis on the importance of the other side (nonsensory: no volume and no weight transcendental) of the HS is, thus, the outcome of *an epistemological perception* of their nature. Accordingly, HS are fundamentally different from the remaining components that make up the human identity. As stated before, HS are impregnated by spiritual/transcendental/metaphysical ingredients that set them apart, on the one hand, from the physico-material world, and make, on the other hand, their action resemble that of supernatural forces. Human beings' transcendental/spiritual experiences through their HS had been known long before the modern Communication/Information Revolution. Modern scientific research has hardly denied the occurrence of the phenomenon of telepathy between distant individuals *(Encyclopedia of Sociology 1974)*. The study of dreams by modern psychoanalysts and psychologists has provided a lot of insights about people's capacity to forecast the future through their dreams. The role of HS in enabling humans to preview the future, so to speak, should not be underestimated (Fromm 1965).

Seen from this book's perspective on the nature of HS, Toffler's Third Wave could principally be traced to the following:

1. As stated before, the crystallization of the Third Wave must not be related only to modern refined media technology. It must be explained as well by the non-sensory (no weight, no volume) transcendental nature that HS themselves possess.
2. The Communication/Information Revolution is qualitatively the greatest of all humankind's revolutions, because it strikes at what distinguishes humans most from all other living creatures as well as from AI machines: that is, *HS*.

The incredible communication closeness that the Third Wave has made accessible to modern generations is a dazzling new social reality that would surely have caused bewilderment, astonishment and maybe madness to earlier generations ... were they resurrected from their graves and returned to the scene of our world today. It is, in fact, quite unbelievable in a materialistic world to hear people speak to each other by telephone and feel as though they are face to face but without their physical bodies side by side. They are also capable of watching the image of the person's body or of hearing his/her voice with complete clarity, as though both the body and the voice are present with them. All these events occur today in people's daily life. This is in spite of the presence of multiple physical obstacles that make the materialization of such happenings fall into the category of *science-fiction events*. Thus, an articulated social scientific understanding of the extraordinary worldwide communicative events would be shortsighted if we restricted our explanation solely to the technology factor per se (as an object) and neglected, in the Weberian sense of the term, the subjective side (the transcendental/spiritual dimensions) of HS. Weber's Verstehen Sociology is surely required in dealing with the hidden subtleties of the universe of HS (Ansart 1990).

THREE MEANINGS OF THE TRANSCENDENTAL DIMENSIONS

Viewed from my HS perspective, the modern communication/ information revolution and its wonders are the outcome of an interaction between the ever improving media technology factor and the transcendental/spiritual/ metaphysical (non-material nature = no volume + no weight) of the HS. Three meanings of my concept of HS's transcendentality may be sufficient to show part of the profile of my transcendental conceptualization of HS.

First, with Toffler's Third Wave Revolution, transmission of the universe of the HS (the word, the voice, the image ...) plunges us into a world of strange and marvelous things that give us the impression that *we no longer belong to the world of the five senses,* but rather to the metaphysical/super-natural world. A second meaning of transcendentality refers to the much extended longevity or even the eternal existence of HS throughout time and space. A third meaning which conveys the transcendentality/ metaphysical-ity/ the spirituality of HS is represented in their capacity to charge social actors and galvanize them with giant and defiant energies that make them resemble, in their power and omnipotence, supernatural beings.

In outlining just these three different meanings of my concept of the transcendentality of HS may allow to say that I have come close to providing an operational definition whose transparent clarity should enable us to ana-lyze those phenomena that are shaped by the transcendental dimensions of HS as already described and as they will be shown in other parts of this book.

HS AND THEIR TRANSCENDENTAL DIMENSIONS

As the thesis of this chapter has emphasized throughout, HS (language, relig-ious beliefs, science, thought, knowledge, myths, cultural norms and val-ues ...) are intrinsically impregnated by transcendental/spiritual/metaphysical features. As such, the know how media/ communication revolution has cer-tainly provided the advanced techniques which have upgraded the degree of exploitation of those hidden subjective/transcendental traits that are assumed to exist already in the original nature of HS. In philosophical terms, the presence of the transcendental aspects in the HS is a sort of a priori presence. That is, the spiritual/ transcendental/metaphysical shades that HS possess are to be considered as taken for granted ingredients. Their scientific credibility in doing social science research can be adequately demonstrated (Hoover 1988).

The remaining sections of this chapter will highlight this credibility or what I refer to as *the other side of the HS.* The most common definition of the latter, particularly in modern sociology and anthropology, emphasizes that those HS are primarily represented by language, religious beliefs, systems of knowledge and science, law, morality, arts, cultural norms and values, etc. As stressed before, HS are to be ultimately considered as the decisive components that radically distinguish humans not only from all other living species but also from most advanced AI machines like computers and robots. There is a consensus especially among sociologists and anthropologists that *language, in both its spoken and written forms, is the most important of all HS.* Without it, we could neither conceive of the emergence of the rest of the HS nor of humankind's mastership on the planet earth. If language is the fundamental basis of the phenomenon of HS, then it should be not only the most legitimate candidate to be impregnated by transcendental dimensions, but become also the main source that predisposes the other HS to have their share from the spiritual/ transcendental/metaphysical effect.

Thus, the examination of the transcendental dimensions of language, before those of other HS, is quite in order.

LANGUAGE AND ITS METAPHYSICAL /TRANSCENDENTAL DIMENSIONS

Proving the identification of transcendental dimensions in linguistic systems does not need a great deal of effort. *Language is the Mother of all HS,* and therefore, it should be more predisposed with transcendentality than the other HS. It may be enough here to identify four aspects that shed light on the nature of the transcendental dimensions of *language as the capital human symbol* by which the human species is privileged:

1. The important role of language in the communication/ information revolution that Toffler and other specialists have spoken of and written about is more than evident. Speedy and instant communication between today's individuals and societies is principally carried out through the word (the noun, the adjective, the verb, the preposition etc.) as the basic unit of linguistic systems. As I have outlined at the outset of this chapter, the speedy transmission of spoken and written words in today's world should not be explained only by the high technology in the field of information/ communication, but also by *the very intrinsic nature (non-material = no weight + no volume = metaphysical/transcendental/spiritual)* of language itself as a top human symbol. With the help of modern communication techniques, the communication by language through its spoken and written forms (weightless and volumeless) has radically transformed our world and made it look like a world of wonders and science fiction.

Communication between people and the reception of the news instantly, despite the odds of incredible distances, have come to mean what we may call the materialization of the metaphysical/ transcendental/ spiritual/ dimension of the human beings' existence. As a result, *dualism of the human entity takes a new shape.* On the one hand, the traditional perception of human nature is that the latter is made up of body and soul. On the other, the new perception of the human entity that has been crystallized by the communication information/ revolution is represented in the fact that the human being is a body standing here on earth, or floating there in space, but he/she continues to exist through the use of language regardless of distance. This new dualism of the human entity puts forth the old metaphysical dimension (the soul) of the human identity in a new fabric. In spite of its novelty, the new fabric remains heavily impregnated by the transcendental/spiritual effect which humans have not been able, throughout their long history, to completely eliminate from their awareness, intuition, rational and scientific thinking in the past as well as in the present (Hunt 1982).

2. As far as the language's capacity to perpetuate the cultural symbolic heritage of human individuals, groups and societies, there is plenty of evidence that attests to that. On the collective level, the written language enables human groups to record their collective memory and to preserve it and potentially eternalize it in spite of their disappearance as bio-organic entities. The Arabic language's full maintenance of the Qur'anic text of the seventh century is a classical example of language's capacity to preserve for good the collective heritage and memory from the inevitability of destruction and annihilation that strikes the organico-physical materialistic existence of those human collectivities.

Likewise, language enables individuals to survive culturo-symbolically their relatively short bio-organic lifespan. Well-known thinkers and writers of all human civilizations and of all ages could not have diffused and propagated in full their ideas, their theories, their paradigms, etc., had they not had at their disposal a well evolved language in their own culture (Parsons 1966). The ideas, theories, concepts etc… - of Plato, Aristotle, Ibn Khaldun, Ibn Rushd (Averroes), Rousseau, Marx, etc. - could not have resisted the odds of time and lived for centuries or potentially forever without the help of the written language. In short, written linguistic systems in particular permit the cultural heritage of people's memories as well as distinct thinkers' ideas, concepts, laws, theories etc… *to enjoy longevity or even eternity.*

3. The new breakthroughs in the area of modern electronic techniques have particularly greatly improved, quantitatively and qualitatively, the humans' chance of perpetuating themselves in a kind of metaphysical sense. The recording of the human voice and of the image in full color through the codification process is a vivid example of HS' ability to eternalize, in a metaphysical /transcendental/spiritual sense, the word, the voice and the natural living image of living creatures and inanimate phenomena. The video is, by far, the most perfect invention that fully enables humans to eternalize themselves culturo-symbolically. With it, it has become possible today to record in a perfect and spontaneous manner the word, the voice's tonalities

and the movement of the individual's body. The late famous Egyptian singer, Oum Kalsoum, is no longer with us today. But she is still with us with the multiple and various poems she had sung with her melodious voice, with her well-known ahat (sad meditative loud voice). She is still, as she really was, with us with her white handkerchief standing before her passionate audience each first Thursday of most of the year's twelve months.

4. On the oral level, language use is also associated with metaphysical/ transcendental/ spiritual meanings. Don't humans of all beliefs and religions resort to the spoken word in their prayers to their gods or any supernatural beings in whose sacredness and eternity they believe? Being skillful in language, the human being becomes capable, on the one hand, of liberating himself/herself from this world's materialistic constraints and obstacles and, on the other hand, of establishing *full-blown relationships with the metaphysical world.* With their linguistic talent and HS set, humans can dislocate the siege of immediate worldly preoccupations. Thus, their encounter with the metaphysical/transcendental/spiritual dimensions in its various manifestations becomes inevitable. They see it in their dreams, experience it through their imagination and closely encounter it in their religious experiences.

TRANSCENDENTAL DIMENSIONS OF FREEDOM, JUSTICE AND DEMOCRACY

The cultural values of freedom, justice and democracy constitute a second example illustrative of yet another type of the transcendentality/metaphysicality of the HS. What we are precisely interested in here is how the impact of these cultural values on human behavior could galvanize it and transform it into a supernatural-like action.

Field observations of both the human species and the rest of the other living beings show, on the one hand, that the behaviors of the latter are profoundly influenced by genetic and instinctive forces. And, on the other hand, that human behavior is primarily determined by the impact of HS. The power of the influence of genes and instincts on the behavior of animals, birds, insects, etc., explains well the persistent general uniformity of their behaviors which continue to prevail among successive generations throughout time and space.

As far as the human species is concerned, there is a great variety in the patterns of major or minor behaviors that differentiate one civilization from another, one society from another and one generation from another. There is a strong consensus among modern sociologists and anthropologists that those differences in the patterns of behaviors are basically due to the impact of HS like religions, traditions, cultural values and norms, systems of knowledge, myths, etc., that exist in those human social gatherings (Smelser 1967). In other words, HS allow humans to have access to freedom of action, choice and difference from the other(s). On this basis, human behavior enjoys a great deal of flexibility. That is, it is governed by *a docile determinism* and not by a rigid determinism as is the case with the behavior of the rest of the living species.

It is no surprise, from this point of view, to see the predictions of human behavior specialists fail in many cases. Modern psychologists and sociologists often tend to ground their expected predictions of human behavior on a rigid deterministic basis whose laws hardly recognize the principles of human freedom, will and choice in the equation of potential influences on human behavior (Philips 1985). It is of great importance here to draw attention to the assumption that the cultural values of freedom, justice and other human universal values, that humans have sought throughout their very long history, have hardly been examined with any serious scientific interest on the part of Positivist social scientists (Hoover 1988).

The positivists appear to have considered such cultural values to be philosophical in nature. Thus, they ought to be rejected outright; they don't deserve a profound exploration as to their impact in the shaping of human behavior. They are seen as metaphysical notions that interest philosophers and not positivist social scientists. This is another demonstration, among many, that shows *the epistemological handicap* from which the modern Positivist social scientist continues to suffer when he/she deals with human behavior which is scarcely free from the effect of subjective, transcendental and HS factors.[3]

The humans' remarkable identification with the traits of freedom, the sense of justice, and the ability to choose, brings them closer to the metaphysical world. In most religions and faiths, gods are seen to be privileged with those characteristics. As such, it is only the human being who relatively shares those qualities with gods. The Qur'anic text makes a direct allusion to that human transcendental link which is the basis, according to the Qur'an, of freedom, will, the ability to choose on the part of humans "... So, when I have made him and breathed into him of My Spirit, do ye (angels) fall down, prostrating yourselves unto him" (The Qur'an, 15: 28-29). With that generous divine gift, the human being becomes *the most qualified being* on earth to take up the full responsibility of its management. "We offered Our trust to the heavens, to the earth, and to the mountains, but they refused the burden and were afraid to receive it. Man undertook to bear it, but he has proved a sinner and a fool" (The Qur'an, 33: 72).

Neither the world of the rest of living species nor that of AI machines has the quantity or the quality of HS. It is utterly unrealistic to speak of the meanings of freedom, equality, and justice among other living species in the same way they have been debated by the human species throughout the centuries. The decisive and crucial factor that radically separates humans from both the world of AI machines and the non- human living creatures is the set of HS. It is on the basis of the latter that the legitimacy of the transcendentalization of human identity is derived. Without taking into account the impact of the world of HS on humans, we hardly can expect to formulate an articulate understanding of their nature and their relationships with what surrounds them here on earth or what stimulates their imagination over there in the sky.

What has taken place on the political and social fronts in the late 1980s in Eastern Europe and in the former Soviet Union constitutes a genuine illustration of the metaphysical/transcendental nature of human cultural values as HS. The changes in the political systems in the second half of the year 1989 and in the summer 1990, in both the socialist Eastern European societies and the former Soviet Union, could not be easily understood without reference to the mobilizing effect of HS on the behavior of social actors. The call by various groups for the democratization of those totalitarian political regimes was meant to signal the desire for ending the state of siege surrounding the exercise of freedom as a cultural symbolic value. It could be said that the politico-social practices of those dictatorial regimes went against the principle that stipulates that humans are by nature HS beings. That is, people hardly could accept in the long run the death of their HS instinct. As argued before, HS are the main sources that generate diversity and differences among human individuals, groups, societies and civilizations.. By their nature, they are somewhat hostile to cruel repressive homogenization which attempts to make individuals and societies identical to each other. Modern socialist and communist countries' policies were at odds with this.

The prohibition to strike in the factory, to travel outside the national frontiers, to establish political parties, to speak freely, to criticize, to express opposite views, to protest etc., - all these practices are in conflict with what the HS are intrinsically predisposed to promote. The strict exclusion of humans from practicing their freedom in the largest sense of the term would ultimately lead to their being very similar to both the world of non-human living creatures and that of the AI machines. My assumption of the human social actors as HS beings first is in clear contradiction with the assumptions of historical materialism (Balibar 1979). The ideology of the political regimes of the socialist and communist societies advocates that humans are first of all materialistically/ economically oriented in nature. Everything else in human nature is either secondary in importance or of false basis. This materialistic perception of humans has led to the marginalization, or worse, to the annihilation of the role of HS in the shaping of human behavior. This is true especially among extreme and rigid materialist Marxist thinkers.

For my perspective, the human being is a HS being by nature (Roszak 1986). That is, in their overall capacity in orienting and shaping human behaviors, HS hardly have an equivalent. Internal or external stimuli to human behaviors are scarcely translated into action before they are screened and checked, so to speak, by one's HS system. This should permit us to explain the logic of individual human behavior and collective social events that have proven able to defy even the most irresistible materialistic power.

The colonial imprisonment of many of the Third World's national leaders in modern times did not prevent them from resisting and fighting the gigantic armed forces of occupation. Their final victory could not be accounted for without making reference to their high morale, whose basis is profoundly inspired and consolidated by the action of HS. Popular revolts in ancient as well as in modern times against dictators and other repressive forces are proof of the tremendous energy that HS could provide the human species, so that they could practically overcome any invincible military power the dictator or the occupier may mount.

The power of HS on social action is enormous indeed. There is hardly any materialistic power that could defeat in the long run the HS based high morale of human resistance. Its vigor and force appear to be inspired and galvanized by a sort of supernatural/ transcendental power. Once the latent forces of HS are perceived in this manner, the transcendental /metaphysical dimension of such cultural values like freedom, justice, equality, etc. would be easily grasped. The societies and civilizations HS charge human individuals, groups, with practically unlimited defiant energies that resemble, to a great extent, the unopposable power of supernatural powers. The famous verses of the Arab poet Abu El Qassim El-Shabbi[4] vividly illustrate that:

> *Once the people desire dignified existence*
> *The Divine is bound to comply.*

That is, when people become firmly committed to their symbolic ideals, they will eventually leave no choice to the Divine but to meet them.

The source of people's will resides, therefore, in their HS structure. When people are determined to defend freedom, equality, justice, their independence and their self-respect, their action becomes like that of the Divine power. That is, undefeatable.[5]

Such happenings have often led people to speak of miracles in order to explain single or collective human behaviors which plain objective causes are too narrow to account for.

The speed of events of the revolts of Tunisians and Egyptians against their authoritarian political regimes have toppled the two presidents (Ben Ali and Mubarak) and their parties in the first two months of 2011. Practically, no body could believe the uncredible fast unfolding of the two revolutions in Tunisia and Egypt. It looked like, for so many thinkers and analysts as well as common people, that there is behind the success of Tunisians and Egyptians *"an invisible hand"* or metaphysical/transcendental forces in my own outlook presented in this book. Similarly, the happenings in the Romanian society at the end of 1989 was considered by many to be incredible. The political regime of the former Romanian president, Nicolae Ceausescu, had a firm grip on the army, the Special Security Police (the Securitate) and the Romanian Communist party. But once the popular unrest and the revolt began to materialize in the city of Timisoara, it did not take a long time before it moved to the Capital, Bucharest. The President had tried to extinguish the flame of popular Romanian uprising by delivering a speech in Bucharest's Central Square on December 22nd. The army and the Securitate's attempts to stop the defiant popular rebellion ultimately failed. The army's shifting alliance with the people had helped consolidate the people's determination for the restoration of the cultural values of freedom, democracy and equality among Romanians.

The end of a whole era of Romania's modern history took place with unbelievable speed on Christmas day that year. The Romanian people's power was armed with the ammunition of HS: democracy, justice, freedom, equality, etc. With those galvanizing cultural forces, the strong power of the revolting, defiant Romanian people had become superior to the military and Intelligence power of Ceausescu's regime. In other words, it had become like a supernatural power that could crush any obstacle that came in its way.

THE IMPACT OF HS TESTED IN THREE CASE STUDIES

In order to deepen the concept of the transcendentality of HS, I would like to use it in the analysis of three case studies. So far, I have confined my self to a sort of a theory building exercise. I may be able to claim at this point that I have established some ground in the field of basic research on the nature of HS. That is, I have raised questions and made observations about their very essential and profound nature. In a nutshell, I have deployed intense efforts to make an inside epistemological reading of the maze of HS.

In order to enrich what I have accomplished on the level of concepts and theorization, I certainly need to go to the field of social life in order to test the credibility of my exploratory findings concerning the use of HS in the comprehension and the explanation of micro and macro human behavior. I confine my analysis to three issues: (1) the meaning of the Arab nation's cultural unity, (2) Canada's Two Solitudes and (3) modern cultural imperialism.

CASE STUDY I: THE ARAB WORLD AS THE OUTCOME OF HS

The history of the geographic region called today the Arab world, or the Arab nation[6] , is seen here as the result of the decisive role that HS have played in the homogenization of language, religious beliefs, thought, tradition, cultural values and norms in the geographic space between the Arabian Gulf and the Atlantic Ocean.[7] The spread of those HS in this vast area came to be realized by the Arab Muslim conquests of that region in the seventh century and after.

The Arab Muslims had basically followed *two steps* to achieve this task. First, they spread their new faith: Islam. In other words, they propagate their religious HS in the newly conquered societies. Second, in a later phase, they had made efforts and adopted policies that had favored the diffusion of the Arabic language among the non-Arabic speaking populations among whom they spread their Islamic faith. This had led in the long run to the assimilation by the newly Islamized populations of the Arab Muslim civilization's HS. A global cultural convergence was taking place between, on the one hand, the people of the Arabian Peninsula and, on the other hand, the populations of those countries which had adopted, for the most part, Islam as their new faith and Arabic as the working, cultural and intellectual language of their daily life. In modern social science terms, the integration of the Islamic religious symbols and the Arabic language and its culture into the basic personality of the large majority of individuals residing between Morocco and the Arabian Gulf created a crucial similarity or a full blown homogeneity between the Arab Muslim mother society of Arabia and the newly Islamized and Arab-ized peoples (Yacin 1983, Abderrahman 1986).

My concept of the Human-Symbolic Soul (HSS), mentioned earlier, helps a great deal in shedding light on the mechanisms and the processes which had enabled the conquered peoples to experience genuine integration and assimilation into the main stream of the Arab Muslim civilization's HS. As pointed out, the HS have a central role in the shaping of the individual's character and personality. An attack on those HS constitutes the most pro-found aggression on one's cultural identity. HS are the individual's soul, as stressed.

To a great extent, this was what had happened at the hands of the Arab and non-Arab Muslim conquerors. The adoption of Islam by a sweeping majority of the peoples of today's Middle East and North Africa meant, on the one hand, their adherence to the HS of the Islamic faith and, on the other hand, their abandonment of their earlier religious beliefs. The Arabization of the tongues of the majority of the population meant also the marginalization or the disappearance of other dialects and languages that had existed before the sweeping advancement of the Qur'an's Arabic language. In sociological terms, the authority of the Arabic and Islamic culture had become *a social fact* whose defense was no longer confined only to the Arab Muslims, but was fought for as well by many Non-Arab Muslims throughout the centuries (Gardet 1980, Al-Jabri 1991).

Familiarity with the dynamics of HS and the rules that govern their action may allow the social scientist to assert that once the religion, language, culture, tradition, etc., of given human groups and collectivities have been replaced by a new religion, language, culture, tradition, etc., the solidarity and the similarity between the conquerors and the conquered would strongly become consolidated. In a modern sociological-anthropological sense, *the Arab Muslim culture has been a significant melting pot for the different diverse ethnic and linguistic groups of peoples* living in this vast geographic zone stretching from the Arabian Gulf to the Atlantic Ocean (Gardet 1980, Al-Jabri 1991).

Christianity, as a religious faith, has spread its religious symbols in many societies around the globe. Its adherents are today possibly more numerous than those of any other faith on the planet. The solidarity between Christians resides mainly in the common Christian religious symbols they share. To-day's European countries, for instance, are Christian in their majority. But their linguistic and cultural solidarity is weaker than the one that exists between the Arab countries. HS speaking, the reason behind this is not difficult to grasp. While Islam spread in both the Middle East and North Africa as both religious and linguistic (Arabic) symbols Christianity spread only through its religious symbols. This is because it did not have a revealed language like Islam's Qur'anic Arabic.

In modern social science terminology, Islam's diffusion of the Arabic language beyond Arabia is a crucial variable that must help account for the differences that exist on the cultural solidarity level between today's Arab countries, on the one hand, and between and their European counterparts. We can speak here of *two cultural states* that prevail within these two blocks of countries. That is, there is a global cultural homogeneity among the peoples of the Arab world. This is due, as pointed out, to the presence of common Islamic and Arabic linguistico-HS among the majority of the populations of the Mashreq and the Maghreb.[8] The Islamic and the linguistico-HS are two crucial variables, not only for the Arab countries' cultural homogeneity, but basic as well for successful cultural integration and assimilation of Islamized and Arabized peoples into the HS of the mother society (the Arabian penin-sula). As for today's European countries they, are culturally similar but not homogenous like the Arab countries. Their cultural similarity stems basically from the common Christian symbols they share. They eventually lost a great deal of their cultural homogeneity with the loss of Latin and the strong and the wide emergence of local/national languages.

To further illustrate the capital role HS play in the cultural homogeneity/ similarity and cultural assimilation/integration that take place between inter-acting peoples of different cultures and civilizations, let's look at the impact of Western colonial experiences.

In the contemporary period, Western colonization has struck most soci-eties of today's Third World. Among other things, colonization aimed to exploit their natural resources as well as impoverish (underdevelop) their HS (Dhaouadi 1988: 219-34), so dependency could be established for the benefit of the dominant party (the West). Most Arab countries were victims of the wave of western colonization. The Algerian society suffered terribly from French cultural imperialism. Nonetheless, the French cultural colonization of Algeria failed to conquer the Islamic religious symbols to which the Algerian people have adhered since the coming of Islam. It succeeded only partially, as well, in the uprooting of the Arabic language and its culture from the Algerian society. The net result of the French linguistic-cultural colonization of Algeria does not permit one to speak with objectivity and precision of total or quasi-total cultural homogeneity between the French and the Algerian people, as some have claimed.[9] To be more fair and objective, one should say that the French language and its culture were widely spread, yet still within limitations, among Algerians of different social categories. But it was a cultural colonization that fell short of claiming that the Algerian society had come near to a complete or semi-complete assimilation into the French cultural melting pot. Full cultural assimilation would have occurred, as explained before, with complete religious and the linguistico-cultural interaction between the dominated Algeria and the dominating France.

The circumstances within which the Algerians had learned French and were exposed to the French culture had also probably aggravated the rapprochement between the two parties (Dhaouadi 1990: 40-56). The Algerians had learned French and its culture in a climate of violent colonization and domination. Such tense and hostile conditions may have played a significant role in independent Algeria's attempt to liberate itself from French linguistico-cultural dependency. This was especially true under the leadership of former president Houari Boumidienne in the 1960s and 1970s (Dhaouadi 1990: 40-56).

The spread of Christian symbols in European soil many centuries ago and France's ruthless contemporary attempt to linguistically and culturally colonize the Algerian society have proven to be of limited cultural impact on the targeted people. On the one hand, Europe's adoption of Christianity could not be more than the adoption of its religious symbols, as explained before. On the other hand, contemporary French colonization of Algeria has caused a lot of damage to the status of the Arabic language and culture. But it was a damage that fell short of their full annihilation from the Algerian society. Islam's religio-linguistic cultural conquest of other people makes its integration/ assimilation experiences in other societies more successful than that of Christianity in Europe and French colonization in Algeria. Using both the religious and the linguistico-cultural fronts, the Arab Muslims had struck the best strategy for the integration and assimilation of others in their fold for a long time to come and perhaps forever. With their Islamization and Arabization, the people of the Mashreq and the Maghreb have been led to sign a sort of semi-eternal linguistic cultural and spiritual religious bond.

In the past as well as in the present, Arab rulers have come into conflicts with each other mainly for economic, political and territorial reasons. There is no doubt that there will be more bloody confrontations between them in the near as well as in the far distant future. The confrontation between the Kalipha (the central ruler of the Islamic empire) Ali and his rival, Muawiyya, took place not so long after the death of the Prophet. The dispute was a rivalry over who was more legitimate to run the political institution of the Khilafah (central government) of the Muslim world. Other conflicts followed suit between the Ummayads and the Abbasids in early Islam. In modern times, the frontiers between the Arab countries have frequently been closed because of political and ideological differences between the political regimes. At times, things got even worse. Arab armies have fought each other on Arab land. Iraq's invasion of Kuwait in 1990 and the military confrontation between Iraq, on the one hand, and the U.S. led alliance, including the participation of several Arab armies, on the other hand, is considered to be the bloodiest confrontation between the armies of modern Arab states.

In spite of that, religio-linguistic cultural solidarity between the Iraqis and Kuwaitis tends to exist in some sort of immunity. This type of solidarity seems to have *its own logic and rules.* It appears to be only temporarily affected by such conflicts and confrontations. Religio-linguistic and cultural solidarity tends to dispose of considerable strength and power like a supernatural force. It is capable of minimizing the immediate costs of tragic worldly events and of outliving them.

The common Islamic and linguistico-HS have enabled the Arab Muslims to preserve their religio-linguistic and cultural solidarity for over fourteen centuries. As stressed throughout this book, the religio-linguistic and cultural ties are imbued by transcendental/metaphysical dimensions. Due to that nature, they are in a position to secure lasting bonds and alliances between social actors. The military, political and economic alliances between nations and peoples can hardly ever achieve such continuous and lasting solidarity.[10]

CASE STUDY II: CANADA'S SYNDROME OF THE TWO SOLITUDES

In Canada, Quebec's desire for separation or for some sort of autonomy has continued since the 1960s to create tensions and conflicts within the Canadian Federation. The numerous constitutional conferences which the federal government has held with the Canadian provinces have hardly succeeded in integrating Quebec as a Distinct Society in the larger Canadian society. The concept of "distinctiveness" which Quebec seeks to legislate into the Canadian constitution pertains essentially to Quebec's cultural dimensions that distinguish it from the rest of the Canadian other provinces. The majority of

Quebec's population speaks French and belongs to a rather French culture. In the vast North American Anglophone linguistico-cultural space, *Quebec* remains and perceives itself first as *a Francophone identity*.

Quebec's call for sovereignty was no longer the strict slogan only of the Separatist Party Quebecois. To a certain degree, it also has become the theme of discussion of Quebec's Liberal Party which was in power.[11] And this was in spite of its well-known federalist sympathy and alliance.

The malaise which Quebec and Canada have had in coexistence is obviously due, to a great extent, to linguistic cultural differences. The larger Canadian society comprises two cultural identities which tend to experience *exclusiveness* according to the Canadian sociologist, John Porter: "The country (Canada) is broken into two major linguistic and cultural blocs that maintain a high degree of exclusiveness from each other" (Portier 1967: 20-21).

Article after article in the Canadian written media shows convincingly that the Francophone and the Anglophone communities in Montreal suffer from the syndrome of *the Two Solitudes*. In their majority, these two groups read neither the same newspapers nor the same magazines. Also, they don't listen to the same radio stations or watch the same television channels. Furthermore, there is evidence that the Anglophone and the Francophone businessmen in this city lunch and dine in different restaurants. The two communities in question belong to *two different poles of reference and two different cognitive maps*. In my own terms, they don't have the same Culturo-Symbolic Soul. As such, the phenomenon of the Two Solitudes in Canada is quasi-inevitable. It is far from being a social fact (un fait social) restricted only to Montreal. The exclusiveness between the two major Canadian communities is manifest throughout the country at various levels. The well-known Quebeker sociologist, Guy Rocher, speaks of the Two Solitudes among Canadian sociologists:

"The Congresses of the Canadian Association of Sociology and Anthropology offer the same scene of a more discrete presence of Francophone sociologists, or to be more precise, of a more than remarkable absence. In reading the Congresses' programs, one could conclude that Quebeker sociology has been on decline since 1965, while in reality it has been in full swing. In fact, Francophone Quebeker sociologists' under-representation is an index of *a profound rupture*. The gap has been widened between Francophone sociologists, particularly Quebekers, and Anglophone Canadian sociologists. A wall of silence has risen between us. It seems stronger and more lasting than Berlin's Wall. There has been no separatism, but there has been instead an effective separation, a moving away and a distanciation. And this, without referendum."[12]

The observations made by professor Rocher and other researchers on the phenomenon of the Two Solitudes are fieldwork observations. They are, thus, of an empirical nature. However, these observations remain rather descriptive, like those made on Cultural Lag and exclusiveness by Ogburn and Porter respectively. Each concept describes its phenomenon, but it says little, if any, about its raison d'être. In sociological terms, the Two Solitudes in Canada and especially in Quebec constitute, for both Rocher and Porter, social facts. But neither of them has attempted to explain the profound reason behind the Two Solitudes in Canadian society. Rocher appears even surprised and angry concerning the deep rupture which continues to prevail between Quebeker sociologists and their Canadian Anglophone counterparts. For him, the explanation of the persistence of the Two Solitudes seems to defy the logic of things. "A wall of silence has risen between us. It seems stronger and more lasting than Berlin's Wall."

The use of my concept of the Culturo-Symbolic Soul allows us to go beyond the descriptive phase of the phenomenon of the Two Solitudes in Canadian society. I have insisted before that HS do constitute all that is most central and profound in social actors' identity. In other words, HS are those elements most crucial to the collective identity of individuals, communities and people. Thus, it is no surprise to see the emergence as well as the crystallization of two Culturo-Symbolic Souls in a society of two major languages and cultures like Canada. Geographically and physically French and English Canadians may live in the same province, the same neighborhood, the same building, yet they still experience the syndrome of Two Solitudes toward each other. They have difficulty in communicating, in understanding each other, in putting themselves in the other's shoes. In my own terms we are witnessing here a *state of rupture between two HS souls*. The phenomenon of the Two Solitudes in Canadian society may confirm some of the assumptions, the hypothesis and the thesis of Symbolic Interaction perspective (Nanis 1968).

As such, the importance of HS remains central both for the single and the collective identity of the individual and the community. Their input/effects on the behaviors of social actors seem to have a transcendental/ metaphysical nature. On the one hand, they appear to exercise their influence in a rather mysterious fashion, like a type of "invisible hand": "There has been no separatism, but there has been instead an effective separation, a moving away and distancing. And this, without referendum!"

On the other hand, the weight of the influence that HS exercise on human behaviors is enormous. So, it is difficult indeed to resist their power, which could remind us of that of supernatural beings.

Put in modern social science terminology, HS play a decisive role in explaining both Canada's Two Solitudes and Arab Muslim countries' lasting cohesive and cultural solidarity. As emphasized, the religious and linguistico-HS that human collectivities may share stand as the best builder of a strong cultural solidarity between them. The case of the Arab Muslim citizen could be a special illustration. Wherever he/she happens to be in the Arab world, and regardless of the conflicts that may exist between the political regime of his/her own country and those of the other Arab countries, he/she is more likely to find himself/herself in *a close bond* with the Arab Muslim individual with whom he/she shares the religious and linguistic-HS of the Arab Muslim civilization.

As to the syndrome of the Two Solitudes between Quebekers and the English Canadians, there is no doubt that the lack of common religious and linguistico-HS between the two groups has played a significant role. While the religion of Quebec's majority is Catholicism, Protestantism is the prevailing religious faith in the other English Canadian provinces. More important, the Canadian society is a bilingual and bicultural society as pointed out. In our times, politically confederated Canadians don't share, as do the citizens of the Arab world, the same HS Soul. Canada's Two Solitudes and the Arab world's strong cultural solidarity are genuine illustrations of HS' impact on cultural solidarity between people.

The dilemma of Canada's Two Solitudes has a long history in the Canadian Federation. It constitutes today a major threat to the collapse of the Canadian Federal System itself. In contrast, Arab cultural commonality has been probably the strongest spring-board that has launched the restoration process of global Arab solidarity after the Arab world's shattering division during and immediately after the Gulf War.

In both cases, the HS dividing or unifying impact on relations between human groups and collectivities is indeed of a long lasting, if not permanent, nature. As articulated in this chapter, my HS theoretical perspective permits us to assert that Quebec's once-for-all successful integration within Canada is hardly achievable. The roots of Quebec's thorny problem within Canada are obviously strongly related to *Canada's dual linguistic cultural symbols*. As such, a Canadian Federation where Quebec is still a member could hardly be conceived without a great deal of long lasting tensions between the two parties in question.

In comparison to the Quebec-Canada case, the materialization since the seventh century of a genuine Arab Muslim identity for the different religious, linguistic and ethnic collectivities that were residing between the Arabian Gulf and the Atlantic Ocean is a good proof of the long lasting effect of the impact of HS on people's behaviors. This is one reason that should explain the slow pace of cultural change that has been analyzed by the American sociologist William Ogburn (Ogburn 1964: 86-95). The great longevity of HS, as elaborated in this book, means implicitly that they possess certain qualities (transcendental traits) that enable them to be in a position to put more resistance to change than society's materialistic structure, which lacks the transcendental qualities.

CASE STUDY III: CULTURAL DEPENDENCY IS MOST DANGEROUS

In a time of globalization, one often hears and reads many sayings related to cultural globalization such as "The cultural conquest of people is more dangerous than the military one". Is this is statement a highly credible assertion? On the other hand, one must, admit that there is a great deal of fuzziness and lack of precision in the use of such terms like "cultural alienation," "cultural imperialism," "cultural dependency," etc., in the contemporary world wide context of dominant/dominated, strong/ weak societies.

All these various terms don't offer more than a general observation of the presence of imperial foreign HS in today's dominated weak countries. The scientific analysis of the dangers of the phenomenon of cultural conquests can absolutely not be fully satisfied with the mere proliferation of such general labels. A mature social scientific endeavor would require no less than the identification of the principal foundations of the phenomenon in question. My extended reference to the notion of HS in this book falls within my attempt to go beyond the philosophical and ideological levels of "cultural imperialism," "cultural dependency" etc., to a more social scientific grounded analysis which could ultimately help deal with the HS universe of the human species.

Accordingly, the ever-increasing critical complaints against so-called "American cultural imperialism," as claimed both by developed and developing societies[13] , have to be understood through a credible objective framework and not through a narrow demagogical ideologically-oriented perspective. The fear of those societies from "the American cultural invasion" may be adequately legitimate when viewed through the perspective of the thesis I have developed in this book about HS. This should be demonstrated in the rest of this chapter.

The propagation of foreign HS means, as I have stressed, that the impact of those HS will be of lasting effect once the HS are deeply implanted into the culture of the dominated societies. Thus, the task of liberating themselves from them in the future will be a difficult one indeed. Past and present evidence shows that the diffusion of language, cultural values, religious beliefs, etc., in other societies and civilizations is the best clever strategy that a society could resort to in order to secure the establishment of more permanent relations with other countries. At this level, there is no doubt that the HS factor is far superior to the military, geographic, and economic strategies.

Contemporary researchers do concur that the French colonization gave more importance than its English counterpart to the linguistic- cultural colonization of the occupied people in Africa and Asia (Calvet 1977: 84). Consequently, it could be said that today's Maghrebian societies (Algeria, Tunisia, Morocco, and Mauritania) suffer more than their Mashrequian Arab counterpart societies from colonial linguistic-cultural dependency (Ruf 1974: 233-78). In my own terms, the linguistic- cultural dependency means the dependency of one's Culturo-Symbolic Soul to the outsider, who may be one' enemy.

As I have repeatedly pointed out throughout the pages of this chapter, the dependency of one's Culturo-Symbolic Soul constitutes a direct assault on the basic foundations of the cultural identity of the individual and the collectivity. In light of this line of ideas and analysis, one should have no great difficulty in seeing the degree of the credibility of the statement: "The cultural conquest of people is more dangerous than the military one." Based on this broad outlook, Third World countries' fall under modern western "cultural imperialism" be it American, English, French, etc., is a genuine objective reality. Today's widespread official and non-official use of English (American) and French in many African and Asian societies does not only contribute to the impoverishment (the underdevelopment) of those societies' native languages and dialects, but it also shows that the struggle to win their linguistic-cultural independence will not be an easy task.

As stated before, the intrinsic longevity of linguistic- cultural dependency means it takes a very long time to get rid of, and this is, provided that all positive appropriate conditions are present in the given society/collectivity. "Cultural imperialism," whatever its origin, would be felt negatively when it triggers and amplifies the processes of the disintegration of the native culturo-symbolic systems of developing and developed societies. Third World countries that suffer from the symptoms of national (or local) cultural alienation, disintegration and loss of their HS are countries which are bound to be most profoundly hit in the basic foundations of their cultural collective identity (Kisber 1982).

THE NEED FOR VERSTEHEN SOCIOLOGY FOR HS

It is against this broad background of analysis that one can come to grips with the kind of difficulty that Positivist social scientists have to face as far as perceiving and understanding the larger implications which HS could put in place for the dynamics of human groups, communities, and societies. In general, the discipline of modern sociology has rejected the idea of alliance with subjective methodology which allows the sociologist to get much closer to the human dimension (HS) of the social actor than to the social structure surrounding him. The modest effort in this chapter has shown that through the use of the Culturo-Symbolic Soul concept, it is time for sociology to fully reintegrate the subjectivo-transcendental components of HS in every study whose aim is to achieve more credibility with regard to the comprehension as well as the explanation of individual or collective behavior.

The study of the HS by anthropologists and sociologists cannot be fairly done without internal comprehension and assessment of them. The need is urgent, indeed, for the invention and establishment of some sort of *Verstehen sociology* able to deal with the complex maze that comprehending HS entails.

REFERENCES

Ansart, P. (1990). *Les Sociologies Contemporaines*. Paris: Le Seuil, 13-14.

Balibar, E. (1979). *Cinq Etudes du Matérialisme Historique*. Paris: Maspero.

Brody, B. (1970). *Readings in the Philosophy of Scie nces*. Englewood Cliffs, NJ: Prentice-Hall, Inc.

Calvet, L. J. (1977). *Linguistique et colonialisme*. Paris: Payot, 84-88. See also: Y. Eudes (1982). *La Conquête des Esprits*. Paris: Maspero.

Dhaouadi, M. (1988). An Operational Analysis of the Phenomenon of the Other Underdevelopment in the Arab World and in the Third World. *International Sociology*, *3*(3), 219-34.

Dhaouadi, M. (1990). In the Sociology of Language Nationalization in the Algerian,Tunisian and Quebecker Societies. *Al-Mustaqbal al- ʾArabi*, *142*, 40-56.

Encyclopedia of Psychology. (1973). Guilford, CT: The Dushkim Publishing Group, Inc., 273.

Fromm, E. (1965**)**. *T he Forgotten Language*. New York: Bantam.

Gardet, L. (1980). *Les Hommes de l'Islam*. Paris: Editions Complexe, and M.Al- Jabri, *The Arab Political Mind* (in Arabic). Beirut: The Arab Cultural Center, 1991. See my review of this book in the issue of *Contemporary Sociology*, *23*(2) (Mar. 1994), 260-61.

Hunt, M. (1982). *The Universe Within*. New York: Simon and Schuster, 315-53.

Kisber, G. (1982). *The Disorganized Personality*. London: McGraw Hill.

McLuhan, M. and Q. Fiore. (1967). *the Medium is the Message*. New York: Bantam.

Nanis, J.G et al. (Eds.). (1968). *Symbolic Interaction*. Boston: Allyn and Bacon.

Parsons, T. (1966). *Societies: Evolutionary and Comparative Perspectives*. Englewood Cliffs, NJ: Prentice-Hall.

Ogburn, W.F. (1964). *On Culture and Social Change*. O.D. Durcan (Ed.). Chicago: University of Chicago Press, 86-95.

Philips, D.C. (1985). *Philosophy, Science and Social Inquiry*. New York: Pergamon Press.

Porter, J. (1967). Canadian Character in the Twentieth Century. *A nnals*, *49*, and (1992) La nation pour Inclure ou Exclure, *le Monde*, 20-21.

Roszak, T. (1986). *T he Cult of Information*. New York: Panthéon Books.

Smelser, N. and Smelser, W. (1967). *Personality and Social Systems*. New York: John Wiley and Sons, Inc., 80-87.

Ruf, W.K. (1974). Dependence et Aliénation Culturelle. *Independence et Inter dependencec au Maghreb*. Paris: CNRS, 233-78.

Toffler,A. (1980). *T he Third Wave*. New York: Marrow.

White, L. (1959). *The Evolution of Culture*. New York: McGraw-Hill, Inc.

Yasin, S. (1983). *The Arab Personality* (in Arabic). Beirut: Dâr al-Tanwir Publisher and A. Abdurahman. (1986). *The Islamic Personality*. Beirut: Dâr al-'Ilm li al-Malayin.

NOTES

1. My focus on the transcendental/metaphysical dimensions of HS intends to revitalize the concept of culture as used by modern social sciences. My approach is, however, quite different from that of Richard Peterson in his article "Revitalizing the Culture Concept," (Annual Review of Sociology 5, 1979: 137-66). Contemporary anthropologists and sociologists have enough emphasized the role of culture in determining human behavior. To my knowledge, they have not dealt with the transcendental /metaphysical aspects of culture as I am attempting to do

in this book where understanding culture's transcendentality/ metaphysicality is considered essential to the understanding of the dynamics of HS and their impact on human behaviors and societies'dynamics.

2. I am well aware that the use of the term soul will be generally negatively received, particularly by Positivist social scientists. The conflicts between scientists and the Church in the West since the Renaissance explain the negative connotations that are still associated with the term soul, or worse, with its French equivalent (l'âme) both of which are widely used by the Christian religion, theology and the Church's authority. I define HS Soul/HSS as the compelling influential forces that HS exercise in the shaping of human behavior. HS are seen as the soul of the social actor, because they are what distinguish humans most from other living species as well as from modern AI machines. My definition of the term HSS does not, however, put an end to the presence of transcendental/metaphysical traits in HS. It confirms rather their presence and their weight in a manner quite different from the religio-theological version. Transcendental/metaphysical dimensions of HS are dug out (carved out), so to speak, following a closer exploration of the very substance of the HS.

3. The French social determinist sociologist Emile Durkheim and the Behavioral social sciences are good examples in their opposition to non-objectivized factors as determinants of human behavior.

4. He was a Tunisian poet hardly matched by any Arab modem poet of his age (1909-34).

5. All literary commentaries concur that these verses of the 1930s constitute a clear call to the colonized Tunisian people to revolt against the French colonizers and secure independence and self-respect.

6. This is often used by nationalist political parties in the Arab countries. The Ba'th Party in Syria today is the best example representing modern Arab nationalism.

7. It is very common in the Arabic language to refer to the Arab world as the region between the Arabian Gulf and the Atlantic Ocean.

8. While the term "Maghreb" refers in Arabic to Algeria, Tunisia, Morocco, Libya and Mauritania, the term "Mashreq" refers to the Arab Middle East countries.

9. This argument may have been used by the French colonial authority to justify considering Algeria as 'un Département Français'.

10. Arab contemporary nationalist calls for Arab Unity by Nasser, the Baïth par-ties, and Gaddafi are basically more inspired by religio-cultural linguistic bonds than by economic, political and military factors. The Canadian federal government's failure to win on 26 Oct. 1992 the referendum on Charletown constitutional accord (Aug. 1992) will certainly not help Quebec's integration into the Canadian federal system. Thus, Quebec's chance of separation has not been removed.

11. The so-called Allaire's Report of Quebec Liberal Party has seriously considered sovereignty or separation as an option for Quebec, if the federal government does not meet Quebec's major demands.

12. G Rocher, "Les Deux Solitudes Chez les Sociologies Canadiens," a lecture given at the University of British Columbia (27 May 1990) at the occasion of the 25th anniversary of the founding of the Canadian Sociological and Anthropological Association. The translation of the French text is mine.

13. The prestigious French medical journal Annals has adopted English as the language of its published scientific articles. This has raised a lot of protest in France. See interview with its editor in Le Monde, 14 Apr. 1989, 12. See also "l'influence Culturelle Américaine en France," le Monde: Dossiers et Documents, May 1981.

Chapter Four

Theory of HS and the Rules of Collective Behavioural Patterns of Influence on People's Behaviors

THE CHAPTER FRAMEWORK

This chapter is the outcome of a number of steps which could be adopted by scientific methods in social sciences. Three steps are used here: 1- field observations of the phenomena to be studied. 2- making of intellectual concepts as seen in chapter II .3- the establishment of a social science theoretical framework and a sociological one in particular.

The steps taken in the unfolding of this chapter are reasonably compatible with the spirit and methodology of modern scientific research in social sciences. For example, sociology believes that there is a strong relation between the invention of *concepts* by the social scientists and their capacity to establish *a theory* on the phenomena being studied. In sociology, the term concept refers to either relations or descriptive properties of things. As such, concepts are not statements and are, therefore, neither true nor false. They simply furnish the vocabulary of a given theory and identify its subject matter. Thus, a theory begins to emerge when concepts are interrelated in a sort of a scheme (Encyclopedia of Sociology 1974: 55). This description shows the importance of inventing concepts for the making of theories and, consequently, for the development and advancement of social sciences and other sciences in general. The Asian sociologist, Farid Alatas, attributes *the state of underdevelopment of Asian social sciences* to what he calls *Academic Dependency* on Western social sciences on which Asian and Third World researchers and scholars heavily rely (Alatas 2006: 57-79).

My observations of social phenomena in various societies have enabled me to identify some of them like: (1)The strict breeding of male animals in the north-eastern region of Tunisia, (2) The full compliance of Saudi male to wear the traditional Saudi male dress, and (3) The collective wide spread custom of drinking alcoholic beverages in Western societies. These three phenomena are part of the long list of social phenomena which I study in this chapter to consolidate the thesis of HS in this book. I use here *two major concepts*: (a) the full collective social influences (FCSI) and (b) the non-full collective influences (NFCSI) on people's behaviors. The former (a) refers to those collective social influences which have a full impact practically on the behavior of *every* individual in the social milieu. That is, no member of the community/society is exempted from the influence of the collective social behaviors. As to the second type of collective social influences, they are influences which have impact on the behaviors of *the great majority* of people in community/society.

As we will see in the text of this chapter, my first concept of FCSI is hardly endorsed by sociological literature. As such, it is a new concept which is the result of my own observations in some Arab societies. Is the FCSI use valid only in the Arab world?

SOCIETY AND CULTURE AS MEANS OF UNDERSTANDING AND EXPLANATION

Sociologists and anthropologists use *society* and *culture/HS* as two hypothetical concepts in order to understand and explain human behaviors and social phenomena. The French sociologist Emile Durkheim and the British anthropologist A.R. Radcliffe-Brown consider society's social structure as the major basis for the understanding and explaining individual and collective behaviors in human societies.

Social structure is defined by both sociologists and anthropologists as a basic permanent system of social roles and relations that help make human groups organized in an interdependent way that resembles that of the organs of living beings (Encyclopedia of Sociology 1974: 70).

As to the anthropologist Bronislaw Malinowski and his followers they have never accepted the hypothetical concept of social structure, but they have rather given greater importance to *cultural patterns* as their significant hypothesis (Ibid). It could be said in this regard that the different hypotheses of the two groups of sociologists and anthropologists are due to the differences between the two disciplines of anthropology and sociology. The former focuses on the study of cultural/HS aspects of society while the latter pays more attention to the social structure of society. This does not mean that the two perspectives entirely exclude the hypothesis of each other: that of social structure or culture. But the difference between them could be identified in this the following: on the one hand, sociologists and social anthropologists give priority to the study of the hypothesis of social structure of society. On the other hand, cultural anthropologists and cultural sociologists focus on the study of culture hypothesis as *an independent variable* (Turner 2001: 135-147).

The text of this chapter will show the main features of the perspective I am adopting here in the analysis of various phenomena found in the Tunisian society and other societies. In all of them I give more credit to the cultural HS factors hypothesis than to that of social structure, without eliminating altogether the impact of social structure influence on people's behaviors. In other words, *I do not give equal weight to the social and cultural factors* as two principal hypotheses in order to understand and explain a big number of phenomena in different societies.

SOCIAL DETERMINISM IN SOCIOLOGY

There is generally a full consensus among ancient and contemporary sociologists that social factors do have an influence on people's behaviors. Ibn Khaldun speaks of man as a product of his social milieu. He believes that man's behaviors are the result of the social context in which he is being socialized. He expresses his remark explicitly this way:

> "*Man is a child of the customs* and the things he has become used to. He is not the product of his natural disposition and temperament. The conditions to which he has become accustomed, until they have become for him a quality of character and matters of habit and customs, have replaced his natural disposition" (Dawood 1974: 95).

Ibn Khaldun's perspective on human nature itself strongly emphasizes the importance of social determinism in which sociologists believe throughout the ages. For Ibn Khaldun, the social influence becomes the habit that replaces the innate human traits with which individuals are born. As such, *Ibn Khaldun* firmly considers *social factors* as very influential in shaping people's personalities and behaviors. This may allow one to say that the expression "man is by nature a social being" could have a new meaning which stipulates that man is first of all a being whose personality displays the social forces of the milieu where he is born and socialized.

This description of man's social nature expresses with full transparency Ibn Khaldun's strong conviction of *social determinism* hypothesis which is widely accepted and used by contemporary sociologists who define it: "The belief that *human behavior is produced by conditions in the social world*" (Encyclopedia of Sociology, 1974: 269). Thus, *sociologists* could be described as *social determinists*. That is, they give high priority to the weight of social influences on the behaviors of individuals as well as on the dynamics of human societies.

It is hardly acceptable to raise the idea of social determinism in western contemporary sociological thought without referring to Durkheim's thinking who had invented a new concept called "les faits sociaux : social facts" (Durkheim 1981: 5). He means by social facts the practiced living patterns of work, thinking and feeling ways which are completely independent of the will of individuals. *Durkheim* considers *social facts as overwhelming forces* as far as their influence on the behaviors of the individuals who finish by adopting and defending them whole heartily. This identifies *the social dimension* of social facts (Durkheim 1981:9). Durkheim is well known in sociological literature that he represents the greatest founding Father in western contemporary sociology who stresses the major importance of the influence of social determinism on people's behaviors. Durkheim's study of suicide is the famous example of this strong conviction of the determining impact of social forces on the behaviors of the individuals including committing suicide (Durkheim 1960).What may draw one's attention here is that both Ibn Khaldun and Durkheim's descriptions of the role of social influences on the individuals' behaviors *do not* mention a reason which explains the nature of the imposing social factors as Durkheim sees them or their nature which makes them able to replace innate dispositions among individuals as Ibn Khaldun states. Neither Durkheim nor Ibn Khadhun refers to the hypothesis of *the role of the cultural/ HS system* as a crucial main factor that determines and shapes the great impact on people's behaviors in society. Ibn Khaldun ought to be blamed less than Durkheim as far as remaining silent toward the hypothesis of cultural influence in the analysis of the nature of social influences on the individual's behaviors. This is because the concept of culture in anthropological and sociological terms was hardly widely present when Ibn Khaldun wrote his Muqaddimah in the late fourteenth century.

THE HYPOTHESIS OF CULTURE AS A DYNAMIC FORCE OF INFLUENCE ON BEHAVIOURS

It may be asserted that Ibn Khaldun and Durkheim's views on the strong impact of social factors on people's behaviors can hardly be understood without taking into account the hypothesis that man is fully a human symbolic/cultural being (Dhaouadi 2006). That is, *Human Symbols/HS* (spoken and written language, thought, religion, knowledge/science, myths, cultural values and norms) are *at the center of the human identity* as it has been shown in previous chapters. Consequently, the absence or the marginality of the hypothesis of the centrality of HS in man's identity makes it difficult to analyze the apparent overpowering influence of social factors on the behaviors of the individuals as well as the human collectivities. Based on the hypothesis of my new perspectives of man's HS nature refered to in this book, it is legitimate to state that man is in fact *a symbolic/cultural being* before being social in both Khaldunian and Durkheimian senses.

CULTURE MARGINALIZATION IN THEORIZING ON THE INDIVIDUAL AND SOCIETY

While I stress in this book and elsewhere my hypothesis on the centrality of HS in man and society's identity, I have found an *almost total silence* on this in contemporary social sciences. Economists and those who have a materialist view have described man as Homo Oeconomicus. On their part, political scientists and those interested in political issues have labeled man as Homo Politcus. As to sociologists, they see man as a very social being or Homo Sociologus. However, despite their great interest in the study of culture, contemporary anthropologists have not used terms related to culture to describe man as first *a Homo Culturus*. This marginalization of the importance of culture/HS and its central and decisive role in helping to understand and explain human phenomena, as found in Ibn Khaldun, Durkheim and social sciences' perspectives, is a marginalization which is likely to *damage the credibility of these sciences*. Then, how it could be expected from these social sciences to secure good understanding and explanation theoretically and empirically of the phenomena being studied? Such a marginalization should reflect *the lack of doing Basic research* among researchers and social scientists on HS which are so central to both the identity of the individual and his society, as emphasized in this work. In the absence or marginalization of doing basic research on the assumption that man first of all is a human symbolic/HS being, it would be difficult to feel secure about the credibility of the theoretical perspective and the empirical findings of modern social sciences. I believe these sciences have not paid greater attention to the most important thing (HS) in the human identity, but they have rather given almost their entire interest to *the less central dimensions of man's identity*. In other words, I may describe the thought of these social sciences as a thought which has given a priori attention to what is close *to the important* instead of giving their entire attention to *the most important* dimensions in man and society's represented by HS (Dhaouadi 2006: 28).

THE INFLUENCE OF COLLECTIVE BEHAVIOURS ON PEOPLE'S

Based on the preceding analysis of the impact of the social milieu on people's behaviours as seen by Ibn Khaldun, Durkheim and most sociologists who believe in social determinism, I would like now to study what I would like to call *the rules* of the influences of various patterns of collective behaviors on people's behaviors. I concentrate in the remaining sections of this chapter on the understanding and explanation of the rules of the influences of collective behaviors. The latter are social influences which have strong overpowering impact on the individuals' behaviors, according to both Ibn Khaldoun and Durkeheim. We will see that the impact of collective behaviors on people's behaviors can be described at times as having practically *influence on all individuals* or an influence on *the great majority of them* . Consequently, I classify collective influences on people's behaviors into *two categories:* (1) full collective influences which touch everybody in the community/society and (2) collective influences that do not affect all members of the social milieu/society. In this regard, social observation shows that people are greatly influenced by the prevailing patterns of collective behaviors which they would easily imitate and adopt. I would like to label this as *the rules of collective behaviors influence*. The features of these rules take various forms and degrees ranging from influencing all or some members of the community/society members of the community/society.

THE FULL SOCIAL INFLUENCE

I define the complete social influence as a type of influence which affects every individual in the community/society. I would like to mention here *three examples* from the Tunisian and the Saudi societies.

1. I have outlined in my studies (Dhaouadi 2006: 269-287) that people in the north east of Tunisia (Ras Djabel, Rafraf, Ghar El Melh, Sounine and Meteline) *do not breed at all female mules, horses and donkeys.* So the breeding of females of these animals is considered to be a big *social scandal/ taboo* that can not be accepted by *the cultural norms* of the community in this region of Tunisia. The well rooted and spread cultural values and norms among the residents of this region have made them avoid calling even the non-living items by female names. The residents of the city of Ras Djabel and the near by villages would *masculinize,* for instance, the female word 'camionette: a small truck' to become camion (masculine). In other words, the impact of the social collective behaviors influence on all residents' behaviors of this region is *too overwhelming* so it affects everybody in this Tunisian region without exception. That is, all residents breed only male mules, horses and donkeys. It is a high scandal in their *local culture* to breed

females of those animals to the extent that the simple mentioning or speaking of female animals in front of them is usually responded to negatively ranging from *feeling shy to violent anger*. Viewing the breeding of female animals as scandal in their local culture is the prominent social attitude among the residents of this region of the north east of Tunisia. Consequently, there is a strong legitimacy to describe the collective social influence on the members of this region as *a full overpowering social influence on all members of this community* (Dhaouadi 2006: 269-287). This example of breeding shows to what extent *HS are very central* in the identity of the community of this region. Their local culture of scandal to breed female animals makes them practically *indifferent* to the existing rules toward breeding animals in the rest of Tunisia. The general rules in the latter see plainly the breeding of female and male animals is something natural and normal. In other words, the power of the cultural scandal against the breeding of female animals makes the people fully capable to maintain this custom/tradition which is in obvious conflict with the common prevailing cultural norm (breeding male and female animals) in Tunisian society.

2. The rite of male circumcision is practiced by all Tunisian Muslim social groups in the Tunisian society. That is, there is absolutely no exception to this among Muslim Tunisian families in low, middle and high classes. The act of circumcision is usually celebrated during the summer. This absolute application of the rite of circumcision in the Tunisian society could be generalized to all Arab Muslim boys in the rest of the Arab World. The sociologist who studies this phenomenon in Tunisia sees there is a similarity between the two phenomena in question here. They are fully spread and global among all members of each community. On the one hand, all residents of the north east of Tunisia do not breed female mules, horses and donkeys. On the other hand, all Tunisian Muslims engage in the practice and celebration of circumcision of Muslim boys. For the sociologist, these two phenomena underline the importance of *the value of masculinity* for the people concerned (Sharabi 1987). In the first case, this is displayed in the extreme feeling of scandal toward the breeding of female animals. As to the second case, it emphasizes the great importance of circumcision as a symbol for boys' manhood. Thus, for the social scientist this extreme strong commitment to the practice of the rite of male circumcision represents *a very strong cultural/HS value* in favor of both the Islamic ethics and the symbol of manhood in the modern Tunisian society.

3. All Saudi men are committed to wear the Saudi traditional dress. Because of the extreme engagement to wear this dress, returning Saudis to the Kingdom from abroad are known to put on the Saudi dress before they enter Saudi Arabia through land, sea and airspace. This dress behavior shows that the Saudi dress norm *does not culturally tolerate* the Saudi male who does not wear in the Saudi society the traditional Saudi dress. This is different

from the male dress custom found in some other Arab Gulf countries in the region where the dressing of Western clothes by men is relatively accepted. As such, the collective full social influence of culture's imperative on people's behaviors in the three cases outlined here may underline *a new concept* which is hardly encountered in the sociological literature. The well known sociologist, Immanuel Wallerstein, does not recognize such a concept as described in this chapter. He says "For we can take it as a given that the norms of group culture (at all levels) are never fully observed by all members of the group" (Calhoun 2007: 427).

This is not in line with the norms of the cultures of the Saudi and the Tunisian societies and the community of the north east of Tunisia seen in the above three examples of my analysis of the rules of the influence of the full collective cultural imperatives on others' behaviors. Consequently the social scientist may have a legitimate question to ask: can the full influence collective behavior be applied on non-Arab groups and societies? Regardless of the nature of the answer to this question, the understanding and the explanation of the cause(s) of the full influence of the collective behaviors in the sample of the previous examples are matters that should profoundly interest especially anthropologists and sociologists. The answer to that puzzle requires a kind of *Basic Research in the cultural/HSl system* and the social structure of human societies. In Durkheim's sociological terms, the collective male dress in Saudi society is so overpowering to all Saudi men, so they can not deviate from it. This may make appropriate the labeling of that as *a rule* of the full social influence on collective behaviors. Surely, the well rooted culture of the Saudi dress in the Saudi society is behind the extreme full commitment to wear the Saudi dress in the Saudi society. Those three examples do give credit to the main hypothesis of this chapter which stresses the strong influence of collective HS/culture's imperatives on the behaviors of individuals and groups in societies.

THE RULES OF NON-FULL INFLUENCE OF COLLECTIVE BEHAVIOURS

What we have seen in the preceding three examples can hardly be generalized to most of human behaviors in society. That is, it is usually rather very difficult to see in most societies *all people conform at all times to society's collective behaviors*. This means that there will always be room for deviant behaviors on the part of some individuals and groups who would not conform to the patterns of collective behaviors in society. This observation is compatible with the common sense view which would say: human societies would not have created and legislated rules and laws that control people's behaviors, if they had not already known that some individuals and groups would not conform. Deviant human behaviors in society are very diverse and countless. To shed light on the non-full influence of social collective behaviors, it is enough to cite few examples form the Tunisian and other societies.

1. First hand observations today show that the great majority of Tunisian women and men do write their bank checks *in French and not in Arabic*: their national language. That is, there is only a very tiny minority who writes their bank checks in Arabic. There are many reasons for the majority to do so. Culture and social structure of the present Tunisian society are two leading causes. After speaking with those who write their bank checks in French and explaining to them that their behaviors is in opposition to the respect of Arabic as their national language and suggesting to them that such a behavior can be considered as a remaining aspect of French colonization after more than half century since independence 1956, I have found out that most Tunisians admit that they are convinced of their shortcomings toward the Arabic language. Despite this, consistent observations confirm that the majority of them continue to write their bank checks in French. In other words, the prevailing collective social behaviors observations confirm that the majority of them continue to write their bank checks in French. In other words, the prevailing collective social behaviors of writing the checks in French persists among most Tunisian citizens because this attitude is strongly rooted in the culture and social structure of the present Tunisian society. The latter has failed since its independence 1956 to create a collective cultural attitude in favor of the use of Arabic with committed pride, dignity and spontaneity. This cultural failure explains legitimately the state of Arabic in Tunisia as described so far. That is consistent with the book's thesis which attributes *powerful role to HS in influencing people's behaviors.*

2. In the post-independence period, Tunisians manifest different attitudes toward Arabic as their national language because of their different educational backgrounds. This could be seen, for instance, among fathers and their children. On the one hand, Tunisian fathers graduates of Zeituna school system have an intense strong Arabic and Islamic education background. On the other hand, their children have bilingual (Arabic and French) education or a predominantly French language and culture education background. This difference in *education backgrounds* appears to have an impact on Tunisians' general attitude toward Arabic: their national language. Observations consistently show that Tunisian graduates of educational system, where Arabic is the prominent language, *are more prone to be committed to the global use of Arabic in their society*. This is true of the attitude of Zeituna fathers and their children. An example of this is presently manifested by the attitude of the son of one of the most well known leading Zeituna scholar and father (Jahfa 2008: 149-158). The son has called for the adoption of the Tunisian dialect as Tunisian national language instead of the classical Arabic. There are at least

two factors behind the difference in commitment toward Arabic among Zeituna fathers and their children:

a. The Tunisian education system since independence in 1956 has, to a great extent, failed to socialize Tunisian pupils, students and teachers to like Arabic: to be proud to use, respect and defend Arabic.

b. From a social psychological outlook, the above state (a) has led to the emergence of *a Tunisian collective attitude* which hardly gives Arabic a priority position in the hearts, minds and usages of the majority of educated Tunisians. This linguistic attitude still persists after more than five decades since Tunisia's independence. In other words, this continuing weak prevailing collective attitude in the Tunisian culture and society toward Arabic should help explain why Arabic has such a low profile among the majority of educated Tunisian individuals, social groups and classes. The sociological concept of social determinism referred to earlier offers great support to the explanation of presence of Tunisians' attitude toward Arabic. This means that the *leading influential cultural and social factors* in society *have a determinist* impact on people's behaviors and society's events. In Durkheim's terms, society's cultural and social structural influences are so overwhelming to ordinary men and women. Consequently, this very powerful collective influence accounts for Tunisian society's attitude toward Arabic as already described. Furthermore, French colonialism is known for its emphasis on the linguistic and cultural colonization, because the latter lasts longer among individuals and in societies in latent or manifest forms. These first hand examples from the Tunisian society show that collective patterns of behaviors follow certain rules in the way they strongly influence both the common people as well as the special social groups like the Zeituna graduates and their children. This sample of examples fairly pinpoints and illustrates that *the role of culture/HS is so crucial* in determining the traits of the rules and patterns of the collective cultural and social influences on people's behaviors.

3. In Western societies, alcoholic drinking is a widely spread social phenomenon. In sociological terms, it could be said that alcoholic drinking in these societies is a collective pattern of behavior of the great majority of Westerners. Because of this, France for instance has begun in the last part of the 20th century to call for *moderate alcoholic drinking* among its citizens instead of asking them to fully stop altogether alcoholic drinking. France's moderate policy toward alcoholic drinking is in conformity with the widespread of the collective alcoholic drinking among French citizens. Paris is an example of a pro-alcoholic enviroment where the names of three alcoholic drinking places begin by the letter b: bar, bistrot and brasserie. Research and reports in Western societies and elsewhere show numerous dangers and physical, social and psychological problems and pathologies caused by the collective alcoholic drinking. In other words, the rational analysis and the

scientific diagnosis of the negative impact of alcoholic drinking for both the individuals and their societies are well established. As such, collective alcoholic drinking is hardly a positive behavior in favor of the well being of the larger community and its members. Consequently, it is rather *paradoxical* to see Western societies continue the adoption of alcoholic drinking as a widespread social collective behavior. On the one hand, these societies are well known for their strong belief in the *rational thinking* of the human mind as well as in *science* in dealing with life issues. On the other hand, they almost put aside entirely the use of rational thinking and the findings of different scientific investigations which could hardly find positive affects of alcoholic drinking for the individuals and societies. This obvious paradoxical situation can be explained by *the rules of the collective behavior* which culturally and socially *condone* alcoholic drinking. In sociological terms, *the culture of alcoholic drinking in these societies supports the cultural/HS reality of their social structures.*

4. In Tunisian society, *dirty talk* is a very wide spread socio-verbal phenomenon which is hardly found in most other Arab societies. Dirty talk is the use of bad words and expressions like cursing God, religion and sexual organs. The latter is called in the Arabic Tunisian dialect *'Sfaha'*. Tunisians and others admit that dirty talk in its three forms is, to great extent, a special characteristic of the Tunisian society among Arab societies. Because of this, the Tunisian authority including the highest political leadership calls for intervention in this matter to reduce the wide spread of dirty talk or eliminate it altogether among all its social groups and classes. In sociological perspective, it appears to be hard to see political campaigns succeed in this issue, because the dirty talk is the overwhelming collective prevailing behavior for most Tunisians in various circumstances. As such, the Tunisian society can be described as having *a culture of dirty talk* (Dhaouadi 2006: 70-74). This is likely to affect the majority of the Tunisian public because HS/culture is very central in influencing human behaviors according to the HS theory being developed in this book or as it is explained by Durkheim's social determinism. Therefore, it is hardly possible to expect important change in Tunisian's dirty talk behavior without first of all establishing a Tunisian society clean of a pro-collective dirty talk behavior. However, this is not impossible for Tunisia. Tunisians have succeeded in creating *a new culture* in favor of wide birth control which has become after independence in 1956 a typical collective behavior of most Tunisian women and men. The birth control program has been very successful which has made the Tunisian authority put an end to it in 2010 because of the low birth rate among Tunisians. As to the reduction of the spread collective dirty talk in Tunisia, it would require as well *national educational campaigns* at many levels and in many sectors of the Tunisian society. The Family must be the first square where children ought to learn not to use dirty words and expressions. This educational so-

cialization should be extended to schools, higher education institutions and the other numerous social sectors as well as the wide social daily life. It might not be sufficient in this regard to just increase people's consciousness to succeed in reducing or eliminating the collective dirty talk behavior in Tunisian society. The adoption of deterring laws against especially public dirty talk habits should help *change the culture of dirty talk among Tunisians*. The firm application of these laws is expected to influence people's behaviors in favor of newsnorms and ethics committed to refrain from dirty talk especially in public.

5. There is a wide spread of almost *total collective social silence* against the presence of *only written French ads* in various places and shopping centers in today Tunisian society. The overwhelming majority of Tunisians hardly protests against these ads. For example, I asked the authority at the Monoprix grocery shopping center if they ever have had protesting Tunisians against the presence of only written French ads in the fruits and vegetables section, they stated they have not so far received any protest against those ads. Such a collective language attitude allows the sociologist and the psychologist to conclude that Arabic, as a national language in Tunisia, does not culturally occupy firmly the first priority place in the hearts, minds and usages of the vast majority of Tunisian women and men. There is *inconsistency in such an attitude*. On the one hand, the Tunisian constitution affirms unambiguously that Arabic is the only official/national language of the Tunisian society. Tunisians strongly believe in this. On the other hand, most of them appear not to be firmly conscious that their failure culturally and socially to fully normalize their relationship with Arabic/the national language is a manifest symptom of what I call in this book *the Other Underdevelopment/ linguistic and cultural colonization after independence* (Dhaouadi 2002). Based on this, Tunisian women and men get involved in non-objective perceptions like their wide spread taken for granted belief that the use of *foreign languages is the way to modernization and progress*. While the matter is different in the experiences of some new developed countries like Japan and South Korea. Consistent observations throughout the world show that societies can become modern through the use of their national languages. In present Tunisian society, there are certain features which could indicate that Arabic looks like it is not the national language of Tunisians and their national institutions. For instance, in normal conditions the national language occupies the first place in the hearts, minds and usages of the citizens. The analysis in this chapter and in my books and other studies (Dhaouadi 2002, 2008) show that Arabic does not hold the first place position among particularly the educated Tunisian women and men as well as the intellectuals of the first and middle classes of modern Tunisian society. The concept of the collective cultural influence analyzed in this chapter could explain the unbalanced collective cultural relation between Tunisians and Arabic, their nation-

al language. In other words, the collective cultural Tunisian mind has not yet succeeded to have a new prevailing collective cultural mind which makes the relationship between the Tunisians and Arabic a normal one. That is, the Arabic language earns collectively and spontaneously the first place in the hearts, minds and usages of Tunisians. In my own configuration, this is a liberation from what I call the Other Underdevelopment. (Dhaouadi 2002).

6. The sociolinguist finds *strange* the linguistic behaviors of Tunisian university teachers of Arabic. These teachers are found to use often French instead of Arabic when they *deliver orally* the grades of their students in meetings during or at the end of the academic year. Personally, I taught a course of cultural sociology to students majoring in Arabic. At the end of the academic year (June-July) students are required to take exams. This is followed by meetings of teachers to report the student's grades. I participated in these meetings in which I was very surprised to see a great number of the teachers use orally French in reporting the grades of the students. Such linguistic behavior on the part of university teachers of Arabic and its literature is *very astonishing* indeed. But, sociological analysis of the teachers' behavior helps make this understandable. The prevailing collective norm among the university teachers is often to report orally the grades in French. As seen before in this chapter, the influence of collective behavior on others is usually overwhelming and allows only a small minority of people to deviate from it. This case of the university teachers of Arabic is an illustrative example. On the one hand, the Arabic teachers have rather a strong relation with Arabic, its literature and its overall culture. Consequently, they are well expected culturally and psychologically to defend the Arabic language more than their university colleagues. On the other hand, like the latter they frequently use orally French to deliver the students' grades. The crucial factors here appear to be *the weight of the cultural collective influence on people's behavior*s in the university milieu or in the larger society as shown in the multiple examples of this chapter. That is, the university culture of most teachers stipulates that reporting the students' grades is to be stated orally in French. This collective cultural norm is ultimately followed also by the university teachers of Arabic. This example and the other preceding ones strengthen the credibility of the central role of HS /culture in the making of the human identity and, consequently, their influence on various human behaviors including linguistic behaviors as seen in this chapter.

THE RATIONAL CHOICE THEORY

My own sociological perspective presented in the previous pages of this chapter is different from what is called Rational Choice Theory in today social sciences. This theory considers *the individual a rational being.* The adjective 'rational' means here that the individual always seeks through his/ her various behaviors to realize the maximum of her/his own interests. Thus, the behaviors of the individuals in society are but the total sum of all total behaviors of individual members of the community/society. These behaviors are always the outcome of personal (rational) desires which are influenced first of all by the powerful urging force of a strong commitment of the individuals to achieve most of their personal benefits and interests. The thesis of the Rational Choice Theory is in opposition to Ibn Khaldun and contemporary sociology's views. It is not as well in line with my perspective/own theory of HS regarding the compelling influence of collective behaviors on people's behaviors as explained so far in this chapter. On the one hand, Ibn Khaldun has given a great imprtance, for instance, to *two social factors* which strongly determine the behaviors of the individuals and groups and the dynamics of human societies. *Al Assabiyya* (group feeling) and *religion* are very influential social forces. On the other hand, contemporary sociologists have pointed out the influence of several forces like income and culture of social classes on the behaviors of the individuals and groups in human societies and civilizations (Dortier 2004: 703). Furthermore, my focus in this chapter on the full and non-full influences of collective behaviors on other people's behaviors does not generally agree with the thesis of the Rational Choice Theory. The previous examples in this chapter show that the full collective influence is so overwhelming to the will of all individuals. That is, the power of the collective influence is *fully inclusive and global to everybody* in the Tunisian north-east community which prohibits the breeding of female animals or in the larger Tunisian society where every Muslim male has to be circumcised. Obviously, these full conformities to *the rules of the socio-cultural collective norms* in the community and society are not derived from innate factors in human nature as the Rational Choice Theory claims, but rather from *the socio-cultural norms* and the rules of collective behaviors in society. This is also true of the non-full influence of collective behaviors as mentioned in several examples of this chapter. The impact of these collective behaviors comes also from *the socially and culturally agreed upon norms* of collective behaviors of the majority of individuals groups and social classes in society. In other words, the origins of the patterns of the influences of collective behaviors are strongly called for by *the imperative of socio-cultural factors*.

THE PRINCIPLES OF THE RATIONAL CHOICE THEORY

Since 1999 two important academic studies have been published on the Rational Choice Theory. The first appeared in 1999 in the journal of *Current Sociology* as a report on this theory when this journal used to be devoted to the publication of reports on the trends of the orientation of sociological thought (Zafirovski 1999: 47-132). As to the second study, it was published as a chapter (chapter III) in the International Handbook of Sociology (Quah, Sales 2000: 50-83). The author of the first study and the two authors of chapter III present the main ideas of the Rational Choice Theory. The first study summarizes the ideas of this theory as follows: in sociology, the Rational Choice Theory seeks to help rationalize the concept of the impact of the rational beneficial economic input on people's behaviors. That is, the individuals have the tendency to seek *the maximum of benefits* through their continuing calculation of the equation of losses and gains. For better precision, the proponents of the Rational Choice Theory define rationality as the achievement of the maximum of things by reducing the losses to their extreme minimum level and increasing the gains to their extreme maximum level. Consequently, this theory conceives *the rational human behavior* and all behaviors for that matter, as mere behaviors which always seek *getting the top maximum of gains and benefits* (Zafirouvski 1999: 47). As to the authors of chapter III of the book, they emphasize that David Hume and Adam Smith were pioneers of the Rational Choice Theory. These two English thinkers believe in the existence of one *universal human nature* whose main characteristics are the following: people's behaviors are the outcome of their desire to achieve their interests and personal goals (Turner 2000: 51). But Hume and Smith and others point out that people do not always act in a narrow way that serves only their interests. Smith and Hume speak also of the presence of the principle of *sympathy with others*, which manifests in people's adoption of the role of others with whom they interact. They may even do more toward them. Sometimes, they do not show bothering behaviors toward others, but rather they act in favor of them. As to the other principle of the framework of the Rational Choice Theory, it is represented by the Behaviorism learning process: people respond positively in a repeated manner to the environment that gives rewards. Usually, people choose those behaviors associated with positive stimuli (Turner 2000: 51).

THE RATIONAL CHOICE THEORY IN QUESTION

A lot of criticism was addressed at the Rational Choice Theory. More space is given here to the criticism made by the author (Zafirovski) of the first study to this theory. The latter is criticized because it considers *the human beings as simple rational ones*, in the sense they always seeks to attain the maximum of profits and the minimum of losses in their behaviors which attempt to fulfill their personal interests and goals.

As shown in this chapter, in order to have credible understanding and explanation of human behaviors we must take into consideration the great influential factors of the cultural/HS system and the social milieu on people's behaviors as my perspective does in this book. As stressed throughout this chapter, those factors constitute the main strong forces that can orient the human behaviors and put them in action (Dortier 2004: 705, Green, Shapiro 1994). This attitude supports the perspectives of Ibn Khaldun and contemporary sociology as well as my view as presented in this work. Here are some of Zafirovski's reservations toward the Rational Choice Theory:

1. There is a big paradox in the thesis of this theory. While the utilitarian approach (gains and losses) lacks credibility even in the explanation of economic phenomena, it is being exported, despite of this, to other branches of social sciences which study non-economic phenomena.

2. The application of this theory in all social sciences makes the non-economic phenomena, as social structures and cultural patterns, look like the outcome of the relation among the individuals seeking for themselves the maximum of benefits in their interaction with others. Thus, social structures and cultural patterns are born. While the opposite view to this offers a better explanation. That is, cultural/HS patterns and social structures create in society the personalities of the individuals as well as the Basic Personality which is socialized to always seek profits and avoid losses in social interactions (Zafirovski 1999: 102-103).

3. The extended application of the Rational Choice Theory on social issues means the movement from the world of economics to the world of social theory. Therefore, it is hardly a surprise to find the use of words like "irrational" and "funny" when this theory is applied in the following social issues: the family, marriage, welfare, people's relationships, color discrimination, social status; political authority, democracy, social movements,, religion and everything else. The irrationality of those theses comes from a *misconception* of social structures and human life in general. These false assumptions *do not make* the Rational Choice Theory *qualified* to be a *sociological theory*, let alone to be a unifying theoretical framework for it (Zafirovski 1999: 102-103).

4. Future sociologists will be astonished from what some critics call "theories of putting heads in the sand" which belong in sociology to the Rational Choice Theory. Looking at the background of both sociology and economics would reveal that economics is more eligible to be attached to this theory. Economics and especially Adam Smith's political economy appeared in historical circumstances which call for *Liberalism* and *Individualism*. As to sociology since Auguste Comte at least, it was a response to the Individualism particularly the utilitarian thought (Zafirovski 1999: 102-103). As far as the second study of Voss and Abraham, It speaks of the Rational Choice Theory as a perspective whose use is increasing in the social sciences especially in economics and theorizing in political science. A big number of sociologists in Europe and the USA tend to use the Rational Choice Theory

(Quah, Sales 2000:50). The two authors of the study underline what they call *"anomalies"* of this theory through empirical testing. In doing so, the findings ofthen contradict the predictions of this theory (Quah, Sales, 2000: 50).

THE RATIONAL CHOICE THEORY AND COLLECTIVE BEHAVIOUR

It is clear by now from the preceding analysis and discussion in this chapter that the nature of the leading causes to the prevailing human behaviors in society differs between *the Rational Choice Theory* and my *human symbols (HS) theory* underlined in this book. On the one hand, the Rational Choice Theory almost sees humans as purely economic oriented beings by nature seeking permanently profits and avoiding losses in all human behaviors in society. That is, these economic oriented behaviors are assumed to be well rooted innate ones in human nature across the ages among humans in all societies and civilizations. On the other hand, my theory of human symbols/ HS emphasizes that the prevailing collective patterns of behaviors in human societies are the outcome of *influential cultural and social factors*. In other words, those behaviors are first of all the result of what I would like to call *the socio-cultural determinism* imposed by the given powerful forces of a given society. This explains the differences in the behaviors of individuals who continuously seek profit as well as avoid loss in all types of human behaviors. Obviously, this is in opposition to the view of the Rational Choice Theory. One can surely argue: if the tendency to seek profit and avoid loss is deeply rooted in human nature, all humans would have been *equal in that tendency* in all places and at all times. For instance, big existing differences in profit and loss oriented behaviors between capitalist Western societies and many other contemporary societies are related rather to the powerful socio-cultural factors and not to general factors in human nature as claimed by the Rational Choice Theory. These socio-cultural factors in contemporary Western societies can be summarized in two features:

1. As I mentioned before, Adam Smith's time in the 18th century (1723-1790) is associated with the call for Liberalism and Individualism.

2. The contemporary capitalist system especially in the American society has greatly influenced the process of socialization of the Western individual (the making of the Basic Personality) in a way that gives priority to the values of material gains in the general wide sense of the term and at the same time it abhors the idea of loss in the large sense of the term also. The outcome of this global socio-cultural socialization - of the individuals, the communities and all social classes in Western contemporary societies – to admire the value of profit and to dislike and refuse the principle of loosing has led to the making of a general Western Basic Personality whose collec-

tive behavior has *a semi-full influence culturally and socially on people's behaviors* in those societies. As an illustration to what has been emphasized, Americans have collectively the tendency that everyone pays his/her coke, coffee and tea when they go together to McDonald, a cafeteria or restaurant. The American expression for this typical American behavior is: *to Go Dutch.* This is the prevailing collective behavior among the members of the American society. It has to do here with a collective behavior which has near full total influence on all people's behaviors. In contrast to this, we find *the opposite* to this behavior, for example, in Arab societies which are much poorer than the American society. That is, individuals like to pay for the drinks of their friends and colleagues. In fact, some of these individuals believe it is a sort of a scandal to see everyone pays for his/her own. In both examples, the prevailing collective behavior among American and Arab citizens in favor of the principle "everyone pays his/her" or "one person pays for the drinks of the friends/colleagues" is certainly a behavior that the different socio-cultural factors have helped its emergence and its wide or full total spread in American and Arab societies. In other words, it is a collective behavior resulting from what I have called *socio-cultural determinism* which influences in different degrees a number of human behaviors in human societies.

THE CULTURAL ROOTS OF COLLECTIVE BEHAVIOURS

The view of Man as a cultural being by nature enables us to understand the weight of the impact of socio-cultural determinism on people's collective behaviors in society in its *two forms*: the form where *all the individuals* are subjects to the *full influence* of the imperative of socio-cultural determinism or the form where *not all individuals* are influenced by it, as I have explained earlier the difference between the two in this chapter. The full and the partial influence of the socio- cultural determinism on people's behaviors are accounted for by the assumption that *HS occupy the center of the human identity.*

The centrality of HS in the human identity helps understand and explain the phenomenon of collective behaviors in societies. Collective behaviors are the outcome of what sociologists call socialization. The latter is a process by which the individuals learn the patterns of social life and assimilate them to become ultimately the basis of the making of their Basic Personality. Human socialization is a complex and a long process that can hardly have an end before death. The role of HS in human socialization does not need elaboration. It is through the spoken, written and sign languages in the social milieu that humans learn religious beliefs, cultural values and norms, myths, rituals, the systems of knowledge and science as well as the two underlined types of collective behaviors. The full success of socialization among the members of a given community/society makes the socialization heritage *a deeply rooted reality* in the core of the Basic Personality of those individuals or a social habit which resembles innate disposition in the human personality, as Ibn Khaldun had pointed out.

In other words, the collective behaviors of the majority of the individuals become something automatic or semi-automatic as a result of what they have learned - through the system of HS - from the socio-cultural heritage of their societies. Based on this outlook, it is more accurate to change the term socialization to become *cultural socialization* because of the crucial importance of HS in the socialization process. So, *HS are the Mother source* for the making of the various patterns of collective behaviors in human societies and civilizations regardless if these behaviors were of full or non-full influence on the behaviors of individuals in the local social milieu or the larger society. The strict full prohibition of breeding female animals in the east north region of Tunisia is indeed a collective behavior resulting from the cultural socialization to which the residents of this region were exposed. Despite the strangeness of such a strict full collective behavior to common people in the larger Tunisian society and elsewhere, the understanding of the nature of the process of cultural socialization through the sociological view can put an end to the feelings of strangeness and wonder concerning the presence and the continuing of such a phenomenon until today in Tunisia. But, as the Arabic proverb says "the feelings of strangeness would disappear when the cause of the phenomenon becomes known". My proposed sociological analysis to the cultural socialization, its nature and means offers an acceptable explanation to the emergence of the phenomenon of breeding only male animals in that Tunisian region (Dhaouadi 2006: 267-287). This phenomenon is explained by *environmental causes*: (1) the extreme small size of land good for wide agricultural fields in this region. (2) farmers need animals to use them to plough and carry various things. (3) the very limited space of agriculture land has made residents choose male animals to avoid the increase of animals by the birth of the new ones which would constitute *a heavy burden* for the feeding resources of the narrowness of agriculture land. So farmers have adopted *the cultural alternative solution* manifested in *the full opposition to the breeding of female animals* which has become a well rooted norm/custom in the culture of this region's residents. This is now the full overwhelming collective behavior of all people in the villages and cities of this north east Tunisian region. In other words, female animals breeding represent, in *their cultural values system, a scandal among all the residents*. Consequently, the full prevailing collective behavior among all the residents *prohibits them completely from breeding female animals*. With this brief explanation, it appears that the process of cultural socialization in favor of the local cultural symbols of this region is the principal source for making the strict collective behavior and maintaining it among all peoples in this region. There is here an obvious support to the idea of the centrality of HS in the human identity and, thus, of their big influence on the behaviors of individuals, groups and the dynamics of human societies and civilizations.

CONCLUSION

I believe this chapter has succeeded to outline *three new features*:

1. The formulation of the HS theory in this chapter and in this book is something rather *new* in the study of culture. Contemporary anthropologists and sociologists have written a lot theoretically and empirically about culture. To my modest knowledge, the basis on which they have established their cultural theory is different from my own HS theory elaborated in the book's chapters.

2. My dual typology of the influence of collective behavior: (a) full inclusive influence and (b) non-full inclusive influence represents *an innovation* in the methodology of making sociological typologies. Immanuel Wallerstein appears not to approve of the existence of full inclusive socio-cultural influence in human societies; while this chapter shows that this type of influence exits both in Tunisian and Saudi societies.

3. My emphasis on the cultural/HS roots of collective behaviors in their two forms makes me inclined to modify the concept of socialization to become more accurate and transparent in its definition of the term socialization. As such, I prefer to use the new terms *cultural socialization* instead of the single term socialization which is widely used in modern social sciences. Cultural socialization, as *a new concept*, stresses the major importance role that HS plays both in the socialization process and the emergency and the continuity of collective behaviors in their full inclusive and non-full inclusive forms.

REFERENCES

Alatas, F. (2006). *Alternative Discourses in Asian Social Science: Responses to Eurocentrism*. New Delhi, Thousand Oaks, London: Sage Publications.

Calhoun, C. (Ed.). (2007). *Sociology in America*. Chicago: University of Chicago Press.

Dawood, N.J. (Ed.). (1974). *Ibn Khaldun: The Muqaddimah: An Introduction to History*. New Jersey: Princeton University Press.

Dhaouadi, M. (2008). *Culture in Islamic and Social Science Perspectives* (in Arabic). Beirut: Dar Alkitab Aljadid LTD.

Dhaouadi, M. (2006). *The Other Face of Tunisian Modern Society*. Tunis: L'Or du Temps.

Dhaouadi, M. (2002). *Globalization of the Other Underdevelopment: Third World Cultural Identities*. Kuala Lumpur:A.S Noordeen.

Dortier, J-F. (2004). *Le dictionnaire des sciences humaines*. Auxerre Cedex: Editions Sciences Humaines.

Durkheim, E. (1981). *Les règles de la méthode sociologique*. Paris: Quadrige/PUF.

Durkheim, E. (1960). *Le suicide. Etude sociologie*. Paris: PUF.

Encyclopedia of Sociology. (1974). Guilford/USA: the Dushkin Publishing Group, Inc.

Green. D., Shapiro, I. (1994). *Pathologies of Rational Choice Theory: A Critique of Applications in Political Science*. New Haven: Yale University Press.

Hoover, K. (1988). *The Elements of Social Scientific Thinking*. New York: St.Martin's Press.

Jahfa, Abdulmajid. (2008). Report on the colloquium (Controversial Linguistic Issues in the Maghreb. *Al Musqtabal Al Arabi, 353*.

Quah, R.Stella, Sales, Arnaud. (2000). *The International Handbook of Sociology*. London: Sage Publications.

Sharabi, H. (1987). *Partriarchal Structure: Research in Contemporary Arab Society* (in Arabic). Beirut: Dar Ataleea Publisher.

Tuner, J-H. (Ed.). (2001). *Handbook of Sociological Theory*. New York: Kluwer Academic/ Plenum Publishers.

Wallerstein, I. (2001). *The Limits of Nineteenth-Century Paradigms: Unthinking Social Science*. Philadelphia: Temple University Press.

Wallerstein, I. (1999). *The End of the World as We Know It: Social Science for the Twenty-First Century*. Minneapolis, London: University of Minnesota Press.

Wieviorka, M. (2007). *Les sciences sociales en mutation*. Auxerres cedex: Editions Sciences Humaines.

Zafirovski, M. What is Really Rational Choice? Beyond the Utilitarian Concept of Rationality. *Current Sociology, 4*.

II

Human Symbols in the Islamic Perspective

Chapter Five

Culture Profile from a Different Islamic View

INTRODUCTION

There are nowadays a number of reasons to encourage sociologists to study culture in order to seek a deeper understanding of the nature and manifestation of culture in the behaviour of individuals and societies. Globalisation has become a hot topic for all at the beginning of the twenty-first century (al-Khūlī 2002:515). In today's world, economic globalisation is particularly prominent. But it is no exaggeration to say that most people on the five continents feel that *cultural globalisation* is even more present. The information and communication revolutions naturally play a decisive role in the greater prevalence of communication, which serves to disseminate the hallmarks of cultural globalisation to all corners of the globe, east, west, north and south.

With regard to specialised branches of social sciences, the study of culture is today one of the most prominent, leading to the emergence in this discipline of a field known as *cultural studies,* which focuses on the study of the cultural manifestation of human groups (During 1999, p.610; Long 1997, p.529).

With regard to the cutting-edge fields in both psychology and sociology, we find on the one hand, cognitive psychology (which is closely concerned with the individual, above all as a cultural being) which is a pioneering branch of psychology (Martin and Rumelhart 1999, p.391); and on the other hand, we find the branch of cultural sociology increasingly prominent among sociologists (Bonnel and Hunt 1999, p.350).

These factors alone confer legitimacy on efforts to devote greater attention to the study of culture and its contribution in order to highlight certain aspects that have been *neglected* by contemporary social science research. As we shall see, these are aspects of crucial importance for undertaking in-depth research on the essence of culture, which is the prime characteristic of the human race, and which has given it pre-eminence on earth and in the universe, as stressed in previous chapters.

SUBJECT AND PURPOSE OF THIS CHAPTER

This chapter is aimed at carrying out in-depth basic research on the essence and foundation of culture from an *Islamic epistemological viewpoint*, which differs from its equivalents in the contemporary social sciences as already underlined. However, that cannot be accomplished without addressing the concept pf culture in contemporary western social science literature, which has been investigating culture and its manifestation since the nineteenth century, especially by means of anthropology and sociology, as seen before.

Such a methodology will naturally prompt us to compare the concept of culture as seen from the Islamic epistemological viewpoint and from its western equivalent. Comparative studies frequently shed fresh light on phenomena that may be difficult for the social sciences to understand explain, and thus help scientific knowledge to move forward. This is the primary goal that the researcher seeks to attain. My ambition here is above all to help to build a solid background for what has been called Culturology (White and Dillinghan 1973, pp.32-33) which, in my view requires a critical examination encompassing epistemology, theories and concepts.

THE VAGUE DEFINITIONS OF CULTURE IN THE SOCIAL SCIENCES

Western anthropologists and sociologists have numerous definitions of the concept of culture. This suggests at least *two things*: either that culture is difficult to define, particularly when using the positivist criteria of social sciences, or that culture is a phenomenon that is in itself complex.

I limit myself here to three definitions from anthropology and sociology. As mentioned before, the most famous definition of the concept of culture was given by the British anthropologist Edward B. Tylor in Primitive culture (1871): "*Culture*, or civilisation, taken in its broad, ethnographic sense, is *that complex whole* which includes knowledge, belief, art, morals, law, custom, and any other capabilities and habits acquired by man as a member of society" (quoted in Encyclopedia of sociology 1974, p.69).

The American anthropologist Leslie White connects the concept of culture among human beings to their ability to imbue things with meaning, which he calls *the ability to symbol*. This allows individuals to understand the meaning of things and also how they were created and how they are used (White and Dillingham 1973, p.29). This ability in individuals is then defined as culture (White and Dillingham 1973, p.9) and there is no individual without culture, and no culture without individuals (White and Dillingham 1973, pp.15-16).

According to the renowned anthropologist Alfred Kroeber, his American colleagues who studied culture and personality *failed to give a conclusive and clear definition of the nature of culture*. In his view, the debate on the matter remains open, despite the wok of anthropologists such as Margaret Mead, Ruth Benedict, Edward Sapir, Ralph Linton, Abram Kardiner, and Franz Boas (Cuche 1996, p.117). Furthermore, for some the problem is not only the absence of a credible anthropological definition of culture, but rather, serious questions about the difficulty of studying culture in the spirit of modern science and using its methodology. Radcliffe-Brown was of the view that culture does not have a material presence, but rather a very abstract presence. On that basis, others like him wonder how there can be a science of something that cannot be seen, since there can be no science based on a reality which is neither perceptible nor visible (White and Dillinghma 1973, p.26).

For some anthropologists, the difficulty of studying culture goes beyond its definition to encompass other important aspects, such as: does culture exist? Where is culture to be found? There have been various answers to these questions. Some authors have claimed that it is to be found in the behaviour, and yet others say that culture is a manifestation which is separate from of behaviour, and there are even those who deny the existence of culture altogether. White holds that culture is located at thee different levels: within humans, such as in their thoughts and feeling, in interpersonal behaviour, and in objects, in accordance with his concept that culture consists of objective and actual events that may be observed.

Sociologists, on the other hand, have narrowed down the scope of the term "culture", which they take to mean what they call the main ideas of society. These include the beliefs, symbols, values and customs of society. This standard sociological definition of culture is current, for instance, in the most US sociology textbooks aimed at university students.

The foregoing brief survey of the concept of culture, in particular in modern anthropology, shows that the notion of culture remains opaque and is almost completely silent about what I have called in previous chapters *the transcendental/ metaphysical aspects* (Dhaouadi 1997) *of cultural elements*, or what I call human symbols/ HS in this book. As already spelled out, HS are language, thought, belief, knowledge, values, cultural usages and myths. In this chapter as in the rest of this work, I use the concept of HS as a synonym for the concept of culture widely used in modern social science. For me and for most researchers in the social sciences, HS represent the main elements that distinguish the human race from other living species.

There is, for instance, an almost complete failure on the part of contemporary anthropologists and sociologists to address the transcendental/metaphysical nature of HS. Only with a small minority of scholars do we find rare and ambiguous terms suggesting that culture is a super-organic human element, as affirmed by the sociologist Herbert Spencer and by Kroeber (White and Dillingham 1973, p.47), or that it is non-biological, as suggested by Tylor, or "extrasomatic", following White or external and "supra-biological", to use a term adopted by a number of sociologists. [1]

These few timid suggestions that culture is a super-organic and super-biological element remain ambiguous with regard to the nature and essence of the HS that characterise the human race. Thing are little better when some anthropologists and sociologists see culture as an "abstraction" (White and Dillingham, 1973, p.24) or as something that "has no ontological reality" (1973, p.26). Given the general failure to clarity these terms, contemporary social science literature is devoid of epistemological theories of the system of HS. The tremendous intellectual fund of knowledge accumulated by the modern social sciences on culture remains content to describe cultural elements without being preoccupied to understand more profoundly the nature of culture/HS by raising epistemological questions on culture's nature. Indeed, most anthropologists and sociologists agree that the world of culture differs from the world of human biology, as suggested by the terms used above. Therefore, culture, as a contemporary western concept widely used in the social sciences in particular, is not dealt with using the transcendental point of view that we find in the Islamic approach as shown in part II of this book.

In view of the neglect and absence of transcendental touches in HS, contemporary social science is hardly objective, in the sense of a cognitive state that allows one to ascertain the truth as such quite independently of the mind of the researcher, unmarred by prior emotions, values, concepts or desires (Fay 2001, pp.202-220). The presence of metaphysical hallmarks, as will be shown, is an inherent truth that lies at the core of HS. The various individual and social factors affecting the minds of western researchers in the social sciences *have prevented them* from undertaking analyses and studies of culture from an epistemological viewpoint that gives full Culture legitimacy to the presence of metaphysical touches. Thus, the tremendous body of knowledge accumulated by those sciences since the nineteenth century offers a deficient reality of the true specifications of HS. Western social science ultimately says more about itself than it does about the inherent reality of culture.

THE CONCEPT OF CULTURE FROM THE ISLAMIC COGNITIVE VIEWPOINT

When inquiring about the Islamic cognitive view of HS or culture, the best way to determine their contours and meet the challenge of their essential nature is to refer to the Koran, the primary source of Islam at all levels. If our reading is successful in helping to understand the content of the Koranic verses pertaining to HS, we shall have acquired *the correct Islamic cognitive view of the nature of culture/HS*. And we shall thereby have armed ourselves with the most valuable Islamic concept of culture, which prompts the researcher to compare and possibly to compete with the concept of culture as used hitherto and currently in Western contemporary social sciences.

My methodology for disclosing HS and their nature in the Koranic text consists of three sets questions:

1. Are there transparent indications in the Koran that distinguish humans from other beings with regard to their capacity to act on behalf of God?
2. Are there Koranic verses that speak with complete frankness about the distinctiveness of the human race from all other living species?
3. To what do these Koranic verses attribute the distinctiveness and superiority of the human race?

Firstly, the Koranic text abounds in verses that accord a special and an outstanding place to human beings among all other creatures, whether spiritual entities, such as angels, or animals that share the Earth with them.

In other worlds, the image of the human in the Koran is of a unique being, who occupies first place in importance after God in this universe. Thus, humans have no one who can contest their qualification to manage the affairs of this world and to assume the functions of sovereignty (vice-regency, stewardship) in it. I restrict myself here to five cases in which the Koran speaks with great clarity of the prominence of humans over other creatures. In al-Baquara (The cow, 2:30) the Koran describes the human being (Adam) as the "vice-regent of God on Earth": And then, your Lord said to the angels; I am placing a vice-regent on Earth". There is little need to dwell on the importance of this office (the vice-regency of God on Earth, to which human beings were appointed to the exclusion of the angels and other creatures on

Earth). As to the absolute advantages of human beings described in three other verses of the same Sûra (chapter), al-Baqara (The cow) 2:31, 32,33, they consist of God bestowing upon Adam *more knowledge and learning* than on others, including the angels: "And He taught Adam all the names of beings, and then presented them to the angels and said: Tell me the names of these, if you be truthful" (al-Baqara) (The cow, 2:31). As a result, God commanded the angels to bow down to Adam alone, as a third sign of honour and distinction to Adam: "And when we said to the angels: Bow down to Adam, they bowed down, except for Iblïs (Satan), who refused and became arrogant, and was among the disbelievers".

Al-Isrä (The night journey 17:70) uses the verbs "ennoble" and "give preference" in order to demonstrate the two qualities of human beings as outstanding over other creatures on Earth: "We have ennobled the children of Adam and carried them by land and sea; We have provided them with good things, and given them clear preference over many of the beings that we have created".

These Koranic verses clarify beyond the shadow of a doubt that humans are special beings who are outstanding and superior to other creatures of the Earth and to angels. The Koranic view of the human race thus represents a complete cognitive (epistemological) beak with the theory of evolution of Darwin and his associates, because the creation of Adam, in the Koranic view, represents *a special case* of creation which is quite separate both from the angels and from the realms of other creatures here on Earth. The creation of human beings stands apart from all other instances of creation by the gift of knowledge and learning that God granted to humans alone. It is because of this strong cognitive ability that it was legitimate to make Adam the vice-regent of God by ennobling him and giving him preference on Earth, and having the angels bow down to him.

Two verses from the Koran connect the angels' bowing down to Adam to God's blowing of his spirit into him: "And when I have fashioned him and have breathed of my spirit into him, fall down in prostration to him" al-Hijr (The recky place) 15:29, Sad (The letter Sad) 38:72.

It is fully legitimate to query the meaning of the words "my spirit" contained in these two Suras because the way the verse is structured suggests that the injunction to the angels to bow down to Adam follows the breathing of God's spirit into him. In other words, there is a strong, if not causal, connection between the act of breathing the divine spirit into Adam and God's exhortation to the angels to bow down to him. As is well known, the word "spirit" in the Koran has various meanings, first and foremost that of infusing creatures whit life. *The Tafsir exegesis* of the two Jalals states: "Attaching the spirit to him constitutes an ennoblement (an honouring) of Adam. The spirit is a genial body by means of which human beings live, thanks to its influence in them" (al-Mahalli and s-Suyuti, 1993, p.457). The celebrated modern Syrian Koranic exegesis 'Afif Abdulqadir al-Fattah Tab-bara' provides the following exegetic explanation of the words "my spirit" in the verse: "I breathed into him of my mower, in other words, when I infused him with spirit whereby he might live, that spirit being of my own doing… fall down to him in prostration" (Tabbara, n.d).

I conclude with the exegesis of Shaikh Mutawalli ash-Sha'rawi, the most famous of Egyptian exegetists in the modern age. He explains the meaning of "the spirit of God" and its being breathed into Adam as follows: The breathing of the spirit of God does not mean that the breathing was done to infuse life by blowing into Adam's mouth. Rather, this represents the diffusion of the spirit to all parts of the body. Scholars have differed over the definition of the spirit. For my part, I think that it is safer not to go too deeply into that matter because the Truth Almighty is He who says: "And they ask you about the spirit, say: The spirit is from the command of my Lord; the knowledge you have been granted is but little" al-Isra (The Night Journey) 17:85 (ash-Sha'rawi, nd, vol.12, p.7, 694).

It is clear from the content of this exegesis that the meaning of the words "my spirit" is quite simply the power of God to infuse Adam with life, of whose secrets human beings have no knowledge, which is why Shaikh ash-Sha'rawi advised against going too deeply into that matter.

Sticking to this explanation of the meaning of the words "my spirit" does not allow Adam the human being to occupy the office of vice-regent of God on Earth or the angels to bow down to him in honour of his special and outstanding nature. God infused not only human beings with life, but also all living creatures. Hence the mere infusion of human beings with life does not qualify them alone to act as the vice-regents of God on Earth. There is therefore a need to seek some other meaning of the words "my spirit" which might strongly suggest the distinctive and superior position of human beings over other creatures by virtue of their stewardship of Earth as the vice-regents of God.

This is where, in my view, the role of the social sciences in helping Koranic exegesists comes in to guide them to the appropriate meaning to be given to the words "my spirit" in the verses "And when I have fashioned him and have breathed of my spirit into him, fall down in prostration to him" al-Hijr (The rocky place) 15:29; Sad (The letter Sad) 38:72. Many contemporary exegetists draw on the discoveries of modern science in explaining numerous Koranic verses concerning the creation of human beings and understanding the functioning of the human brain and body, and especially the relationship of human beings to natural phenomena in the universe, such as the sun, the moon, stars, mountains, seas, volcanoes and earthquakes, all of which have served to reinforce the idea of *the unimitability* (I'jaz) of the Koran. There are increasing numbers of publications, symposia and conferences in this field in the modern Islamic world. We agree in this respect with

Dr Zaghlul an-Najjar, who stresses that it is not possible to understand many Koranic verses without relying on highly credible scientific discoveries concerning human beings and natural phenomena of the universe. In the same way and to the same extent, modern exegetists are also called upon to make use of the fund of contemporary social science learning concerning the understanding of the behviour of individuals and communities, and the dynamism of societies and human cultural hallmarks. These disciplines certainly help to get closer to the meaning of the words "my spirit" in the verses referred to above. The disciplines of anthropology, sociology and psychology all agree that human beings are distinct from other beings by virtue of what those disciplines call culture or what I have termed HS which have qualified humans in the past, and continue to do so in the present and future, to play the role of vice-regent of God on Earth. In other words, the phrase "I have breathed of my spirit" means that the divine breathing into Adam is first and foremost *a cultural/HS breathing* in the contemporary sense given by the social sciences to the term culture. The breathing of HS into Adam alone conferred upon him, to the exclusion of others, the function of the stewardship of Earth, and the attendant bowing down of the angels to him. Such a cultural reading of the words "my spirit" in these verses makes clear just how much enhanced credibility the explanation of Koranic verses has if exegetists draw on modern scientific knowledge.

THE COGNITIVE KORNAIC FOUNDATIONAL VIEW OF CULTURE

It is clear from the foregoing that the Koran has a cognitive (epistemological) view concerning HS as a distinctive feature of the human race. The divine cultural breathing into Adam, to the exclusion of others, is thus a breathing that has, according to the Koranic view, *metaphysical roots and a metaphysical nature*. Its source is not the world of Earth, but rather the world of the heavens, of which the creatures of Earth were deprived, and which was given to human beings alone. The Koran speaks with complete frankness of the metaphysical nature of the cultural breathing for which human beings alone were singled out: "And when I have fashioned him and have breathed of my spirit into him, fall down in prostration to him". In other words, the cultural breath deep within Adam comes from the divine essence itself. There is thus no room in the Koranic vision for doubt about the essential metaphysical nature of HS that distinguish the human race from other living species.

On the other hand, as noted, most Western social science literature is almost completely *silent* about the metaphysical/transcendental aspects of culture. It studies and analyses the cultures of societies using a descriptive or positivist method without bothering to raise cognitive (epistemological) questions about the nature of culture as a unique hallmark of individual humans and of human societies, shying away from examining the features of things that are not subject to the world of sensory perception or quantity. It is an objective, scientific failing to reject the metaphysical despite its strong presence at the heart of HS, one that restricts understanding of the behaviour of individuals and the dynamism of societies and civilisations. How can one have confidence in the findings of social science research, which studies culture stripped – for reasons of epistemology- of its essential metaphysical hallmarks? Hence, the western social sciences should not merely study the religious factors involved in understanding the behaviour of individuals and the dynamics of societies (Heath, 2000), but also draw on the cognitive (epistemological) vision of religions as a source of scientific understanding (Ebaugh, 2002), as this study endeavours to highlight with respect to culture.

HS have a transcendental/ metaphysical character that makes them different from the components of the human body and the material world. Individuals thus have a dual identity: a system of HS, on the one hand, and organic biological and physiological elements, on the other hand. It is the HS that are the most prominent and decisive in the determination of the identity of individuals, and hence their behaviour. The five most important transcendental/ metaphysical traits are as follows.

1. HS do not have *weight and volume*, unlike the biological and physiological components of living creatures and the material world.

2. As a direct consequence, HS enjoy ease and rapidity of transmission over time and space as explained before.

3. HS are undiminished by sharing, unlike elements of the material world. If we give others something from our knowledge, learning thought, creed, cultural values, language, and so on we lose nothing.

4. HS have a great capacity to survive for long periods of time in human societies. Indeed, through written language, their longevity may even be indefinite. The thought of Akhenaton, Socrates, Aristotle, Ibn Rushd (Averroes), al-Ghazali, Ibn Khaldun, Rousseau, Descartes, Hume and other thinkers and scholars would not have survived or enjoyed such a long period of survival if it had not been recorded in the letters and words of the varied languages that enable it to meet the challenge of immortality. Languages have a particularly prominent role to play with regard to the preservation and immortalisation of the collective heritage of human communities. Written languages, especially, enable human communities to record, preserve and immortalise their collective memory despite the extinction of those communities' organic and biological presence as living organisms; despite their changes of place and the fact that successive generations of their members live in different ages from their own. The complete preservation of the language of the thad (a letter/sound thought to be unique to Arabic) in the Koranic text is a prime example of the capacity of the language of the

immortal text to safeguard the collective memory and heritage from the oblivision that is brought about by the passage of time, changes in the environment, and the temporary nature of corporeal organic biological existence.

These transcendental/metaphysical dimensions are not limited to written language alone. The oral use of language is also coupled with transcendental and metaphysical meanings. Humankind's encounter with the metaphysical dimension in its various manifestations thus becomes inevitable: individuals see it in their dreams, it fills their imagination and they encounter it at close quarters in their religious experiences.

5. HS posses an extraordinary power to imbue individuals and societies with enormous energy, enabling those who possess it to triumph over the greatest challenges, in all their many forms. By way of example, the values of freedom, justice and equality have been shown, over the long course of human history, to be HS capable of endowing individuals and communities with colossal, surging energy similar, to some extent, to overwhelming metaphysical forces which no one can withstand. Such is what the words of the Tunisian Arab poet, Abu l-Qasim ash-Shabi, suggest: "If, one day the people choose to live degnified, fate must inevitably respond positively". The source of peoples' real volition lies in the world of HS. That is, when people unite to defend freedom, equality, justice and other human values, and their right to independence and self-respect, their reaction becomes like the reaction of fate, "which neither preserves anything nor leaves anything behind". This explains why people resort to talking of miracles in respect of certain individual or collective events, which enter the historical record despite the lack of concrete evidence for them. They are manifestations of the decisive impact of HS in giving birth and momentum to people's behaviour in human societies and civilizations throughout the ages. These points about human HS possessing, in the Koranic view, metaphysical roots needs to be made more concrete in the world of human and social reality so that the metaphysical features of HS may be used in current field research in the social sciences. The transformation of the abstract notion of the metaphysics of HS to a down-to-earth formulation of the manifestations of their metaphysical features provides a procedural concept that social science researchers may use in the core of their fieldwork and theoretical research. This procedural concept contributes to beginning the reconciliation of all non-objective factors influencing the behaviour of the individual and society, which the positivist view, in particular, avoids taking into account in understanding and explaining collective and individual phenomena. The remainder of this chapter deals with some of the implications of this perspective.

THE FEATURES OF SOME OF THE TRANSCENDENTAL ASPECTS IN HS

It is not sufficient here to affirm that HS are a central part of the breathing of the divine cultural spirit into human beings. We need to clarify how the breathing or insufflation of the divine cultural spirit manifests itself in certain HS. We shall present here three examples of HS that reflect some features of aspects of the insufflation of the divine cultural spirit.

LANGUAGE AND ITS METAPHYSICAL TRAITS

The Koran affirms the eternal nature of the divine essence. "He is the First and the Last" (al-Hadid (The iron) 57:3). "Everyone on Earth must pass away; there shall remain but the face of your Lord, full of glory and munificence" (ar-Rahman (The merciful) 55:26-27). Several HS are also described as being long lasting or even eternal. Building on the points made in the previous section, let us briefly consider language as the most important of all HS to see how it is able to prolong or immortalize the life of individuals and human societies.

It is not difficult to establish the features of metaphysical touches in linguistic structures, for language as *the Mother of HS* (White 1959). As such, language is better suited than other elements to carry flashes of the Islamic cognitive view of the world of HS. It is possible to confine ourselves to mentioning and defining four features in respect of the identification of the metaphysical features of language as a cultural symbol by which the human race is distinguished.

1. The place occupied by language in the information revolution, which Toffler and other experts in this field speak about, is well known. The speed of instant communication, carried out in the twinkling of an eye between individuals and societies today is achieved basically by means of the primary unit, which is the linguistic structure as represented by the word (such as the noun, adjective, verb, particle, number and symbol). The speed of transmission of the written and spoken word in today's world is not only attributable to modern communication technologies, but is also profoundly influenced by the nature of language itself, as humankind's most important HS. Communication by means of language, in both written and spoken form, has radically transformed our world and improved communication technologies such as telephone, fax, and the Internet, have endowed it with the qualities to wonder and marvel at. Human communication and instant news gathering has, despite the enormous distances, become imbued with what we might term the metaphysical dimension of human existence in this world, from which a new expression of the duality of human existence takes shape. The conventional

formulation of the nature of human beings consists in their having a body and a soul. Under the new conception of human existence, crystallized by the information revolution, human beings are bodies, either reposing on the earth's surface or floating in space, but interconnected and present there by means of language at incredible distances either on Earth or in the vastness of space. *This new type of duality* casts the old metaphysical aspect of human identity (the spirit) in a new guise which, despite its novelty, continues to have strong links to the world of the metaphysical and the intangible, which human beings have been unable, in general, throughout their long history, to eliminate entirely from their perception, intuition and intellectual and scientific thinking (Hunt 1982, pp.315-353).

2. Field data confirm the power of *language to immortalize individuals and groups symbolically, across time and space.* At the collective level, written language in particular enables human groups to record, preserve and immortalize their collective memory, despite the evanescence of their organic and biological existences as groups and despite the possibility of subsequent generations changing their location and mode of life in later times. It is the same with individuals, great writers in particular (Parsons 1966). In short, our linguistic structure permits the stock of a people's memory and the ideas of outstanding individuals to enjoy a greater or lesser degree of the features of immortality and the eternal.

3. The capacity of HS to enable individuals to enjoy a kind of immortality has improved thanks to successive technological discoveries in the filed of advanced electronics. The recording of sound and color images by the process of digitization is a lively example of the ability of HS to immortalize the words, sounds and live, natural images of living beings and Culture Profile from a Different Islamic View inanimate phenomena.

4. At the cultural level the use of language is also coupled with *metaphysical meanings.* Do individuals of all creeds and religions not use the spoken word in their existential reflections, their supplications and entreaties to their god or to whatever else they believe to be eternal or holy? Set apart from other living beings by language, human beings are able to liberate themselves from the physical constraints of this world and establish relations and links with the metaphysical world. Through its linguistic ability, humankind succeeds in disengaging from worldly and momentary concerns.

HS THAT IMBUE HUMAN BEINGS WITH GREAT ENERGY

Therefore, neither the world of animals and beasts nor the world of machines and devices endowed with modern artificial intelligence enjoys the quantity and quality of the nature of the world of HS possessed by human beings.

A representative example, perhaps, of the metaphysical dimensions of the world of values as HS is the *al-Aqsa intifada* waged since 28 September 2000 by the Palestinian Arab people against Israeli occupation and settlement in order to liberate their land to achieve justice and equality.

Faced with overwhelming Israeli superiority in military equipment the Palestinians have adopted new methods of resistance. The al-Aqsa intifada is, like its predecessor in 1989, called the "revolution of the stones", because it is with pebbles and stones that Palestinian children and youths face heavily armed Israeli occupation army. The second innovative strategy consists in young Palestinians turning themselves into human bombs against the Israeli military and the civilian population inside Israel itself. Finally, the Palestinians also fight on Israeli-occupied land with conventional weapons, resisting settlers and the occupation forces with weapons an material that are limited in comparison with the lethal modern weaponry possessed by the opposing forces.

The pressing cognitive question that must be asked is: what are the decisive factors that have resulted in the phenomena of the Intifida, its means of resistance and its continuation for a not inconsiderable period of time, despite the fact that the Israeli State has assassinated the leaders of the Palestinian resistance, committed numerous massacres in the towns and villages of Palestine and sought to destroy the mainstays of the infrastructure of Palestinian society? There is little doubt that resistance with pebbles and stones against an army equipped with tanks and lethal modern weaponry is military and physically unrealistic. The matter is much worse with regard to those Palestinians who have chosen certain death by turning themselves into human bombs against the occupation. The motives and driving forces for such Palestinian behaviour in combat are certainly not material. They are, rather, high moral forces rooted in the system of Palestinian HS. As outlined in this book, human beings are by nature the bearers of HS. This is what explains the logic of individual behaviour and collective actions, which have a proven ability to defy overwhelming physical facts, as we have seen from the example of the Palestinian intifada. The resistance of Third World liberation movements in the last century is further testimony to the credibility of the capacity of HS to create, drive and orient individual and collective human behaviour towards goals that, materially, seem extremely difficult or impossible to achieve. The imprisonment of many Third World leaders in the modern era did not prevent them from fighting to withstand the vastly more powerful material forces of the colonizer. There is no more credible explanation for their final victory over the occupiers than the factor of their being armed with moral weapons or the weapons of the world of HS, in accordance with my concept of HS in this chapter. Popular uprisings against oppressors in ancient and modern times merely demonstrate the importance of the ammunition that human beings may derive from the world of HS, which transform those individuals' energy into a challenge to the greatest military force the tyrant or colonizer may possess.

TOWARDS SOCIOLOGY OF THE METAPHYSICS OF HS

It is clear from the preceding pages of this chapter that we are in the process of establishing what we might call sociology of the metaphysics of HS on an Islamic epistemological foundation. I have derived the metaphysics of HS, on the one hand, from methodological analysis of the nature of HS themselves, and on the other hand, by employing the Islamic epistemology of HS. As such, my vision in this chapter and others represents a theoretical framework with cultural foundations and an Islamic epistemology. It is thus a perspective that differs completely from the positivist one. This new view of HS responds strongly to the growing calls from sociologists to integrate and draw on religion to understand and explain the phenomena under study and establish theoretical thinking at the heart of these sciences (Ebaugh, 2002).

1. The careful study of the essence of HS must the included in the category of basic scientific research. HS, as we have seen, represent the essence of human beings. There is, therefore, little doubt that uncovering their nature and secrets is a priority, as a deep understanding of HS is conducive to helping us to better understand individual behaviour and the dynamics of human society.

2. My choice of *the Islamic HS/ cultural perspective* for studying the metaphysical features of the system of cultural values stems, on the one hand, from the lack of interest and failure of the positivist and other perspectives to investigate this topic, as I have shown in this chapter and elsewhere. On the other hand, my approach is at the cutting edge, concretizing the embedding of religious thought at the heart of the social sciences. In my view, what is important for the advancement of science is not stubborn adherence to a particular perspective and methodology, but using the appropriate perspective and methodology to understand and explain the phenomenon under consideration. There is, then, strong legitimacy for adopting the *Islamic cultural perspective as an alternative* to the conventional positivist perspective, the principles of which were established in the nineteenth century, and which, in the view of many sociologists today, is no longer adequate. These scholars believe that the time has come for these fundamental changes at the heart of sociology.

Sociologists need to be convinced that there is no single scientific methodology for research in the social sciences. There is a call today to legitimate diversity among the scientific methods that sociologists may employ to study phenomena of interest to them (Risman and Tomaskovic-Devey 1998).

This new approach among sociologists holds that sociology is able to adopt and employ a range of intellectual and theoretical frameworks without thereby prejudicing its central vision (Risman and Tomaskovic-Devey 1998, p.10). My perspective thus remains faithful, in respect of its object of study, to the core of sociology. This part of this chapter focuses its analysis on the system of HS that have always had priority in sociological and anthropological studies. What makes this chapter particularly faithful to sociology and anthropology is its attempt to impart a new scientific character to the understanding of the system of HS through its focus on their metaphysics, derived from the cognitive view and from the metaphysical observations of Islam. Discovering the metaphysical manifestation in the system of HS justifies what was missing at the core of the cognitive stock of modern sociology and anthropology, and our understanding is thereby completed of the most important traits that distinguish the members of the human race from other species.

This new generation of sociologists believes that sociology is a science that is characterized epistemologically by *creativity and innovation* which qualifie it to be at the cutting edge in proposing new ways of conducting scientific activity. What is important in this regard is not the adoption of a particular method of scientific research, but rather the use of a methodology that is actually capable of building a solid scientific structure. This must first of all be capable of identifying the social and cultural factors that underlie the genesis of the phenomenon under consideration, since the explanation of phenomena by means of social and cultural influences is incorporated into the heart of the sociological perspective. This is *what distinguishes the sociological perspective* from both the psychological and the biological perspectives in their explanation of human behaviour. Whatever research methodology we choose must have as its ultimate goal the discovery of the cause or causes that have contributed and are contributing to the formation and genesis of the phenomenon. However, the search for the causal factors of social phenomena should not be limited to the quantitative factors stressed by positivism since the nineteenth century. Rather, the search for the causes of social phenomena must also aspire to identify *qualitative causes*, which positivism has not sought to use. Comparing it with the perspective of western sociology, my perspective in this chapter could be placed under the heading of what the American sociologist Randall Collins (1982) has called *"non-obvious sociology"*, from which uncovers hidden processes behind the obvious. It is a discipline that demonstrates that obvious matters are not necessarily the most significant.

My use of the Islamic cultural perspective, based upon the metaphysical epistemology of HS, is a new type of paradigm for social scientific research. What I have endeavored to do in this chapter and in this book as a whole is to define *a new method* for scientific work on what is hidden from the gaze of most contemporary sociologists and anthropologists in their studies of culture/HS. It gives sociology a touch of creativity, allowing it, as a science, to be innovative in its capacity to define new methods of scientific research.

THE HARMONIZATION OF MY PERSPECTIVE WITH REFLEXIVE SOCIOLOGY

There is little doubt that the Islamic cultural perspective proposed here for the study of culture is one which brings together a number of cognitive viewpoints constituted essentially by sociology, philosophy and religion. This is a formula that is rejected by conventional positivist science but is accepted and welcomed by *the new trend* at the heart of sociology (Bunge 1999; Risman and Tomaskovic-Devery 1998). Furthermore, the sociology called for by Pierre Bourdieu supports, to a large extent, our approach in this chapter. Bourdieu's cognitive intellectual project, termed "reflexive (self-critical) sociology" (Bourdieu and Wacquant 1992, pp.43-70), has little respect of the boundaries drawn between cognitive specializations (Bourdieu and Wacquant 1992, p.13). Hence, this sociology calls for new methods to be devised that are conductive to understanding and explaining social phenomena with a high degree of credibility. It thus represents a challenge to the current divisions and patterns of thought that are prevalent in the social sciences. Bourdieu urges the adoption and use of *multiple methodologies* in the study of social phenomena and in the research carried out by sociologists (Bourdieu and Wacquant 1992, p.32). He believes that sociology, as a cognitive view, needs to be a total science (Bourdieu and Wacquant 1992, p.30). In the words of Marcel Mauss, sociology must provide us with *the total social fact* capable of restoring the basic unity of scientific research, which has long been torn apart by the boundaries between cognitive specializations, empirical fields and techniques of observation and analysis. On this basis, Bourdieu is vehemently opposed to separating methodological field work from theory in sociology, defining méthodologisme as the tendency of the research to separate the intellectual effort required to devise methodologies from their profitable use in scientific work itself. Bourdieu believes that mastery of research techniques often results in poverty of sociological theorizing regarding the phenomenon under consideration. True sociology, then, is that which always preserves the strong link between method and thought (Bourdieu and Wacquant 1992, pp.31-32).

Bourdieu concludes from his defence of a reflexive, self-critical sociology that such an approach is not the enemy of the modern scientific view, but that it does go against numerous positivist conceptions of the social sciences, and also against the absolute separation introduced by the positivist social sciences between the quantitative and qualitative aspects of the phenomena studied (Bourdieu an Wacquant 1992, p.39). It is thus evident that this model of sociology urges a linkage and dialogue between both sides of the duality, in respect of both the phenomenon studied and sociological practice. The latter must, on the one hand, give priority to the study of both the qualitative and the quantitative aspects of the social phenomenon, and on the other hand, open a dialogue between field work and theoretical work to address the challenge of understanding and explaining social phenomena and processes.

From the above, it may be said that *my alternative* Islamic cultural perspective on the study of culture falls within the kind of sociology called for by Bourdieu and others (Bourdieu an Wacquant 1992, pp.43-70). We sharply criticize contemporary western sociology, which almost completely ignores the metaphysical features of HS, some of which I have mentioned in this chapter. Instead, I call today upon Muslim sociologists to desist from merely imitating their western counterparts, both past and present, with respect to epistemology, methodology and theory. Western sociology today suffers from *a crisis of epistemological unity*, which Wallerstein (1999, pp.1-16) has urged all sociologists to overcome. Sociologists in the Islamic world are fully qualified to respond to this pressing call and implement it in Islamic sociological thought in the twenty first century. The perspective of Islamic culture is at the cutting edge in his field: the unity of all knowledge and sciences. Consequently, there is no place in this culture for the phenomenon of *two cultures* and antipathy and hostility between cognitive and scientific specializations. In other words, Islamic sociology, based on the power of the absolute, unifying epistemology of human knowledge, is well placed to be wholly impervious to the epistemological crisis that western sociology and other types of knowledge and science are experiencing today.

The study of culture or HS from the Islamic cultural perspective is entirely legitimate in relation to Islamic sociology, as this book's chapters make clear. On the one hand, it will contribute to rooting this discipline in the perspective and epistemology of the mother culture of Islamic societies, and on the other hand, the metaphysical features of HS will help to open new, previously unclear, cognitive horizons in the legacy of contemporary sociological thought on culture – that enormous, complex whole, in the words of Tylor.

REFERENCES

Al-Ansari, M.J. (2001). Mas Uliya min… tajdid al-fikr al-arabi…? (Responsibility for… the Renewal of Arab Thought …? *Al-Bahrain ath-thaqafiya* (Cultural Bahrain), *30*, 140-144.

Al-Khuli, Usama, A. 2000. Al-Arab wa Alawlama (Ehe Arabs and Globalization) 3rd edn. Beirut, Center for Arab Unity Studies.

Al Mahalli Jalal Ad-Din Ibn A. and S.Suyuti, Jalal Ad-Din. (1993). Abdurahman Ibn Abi. *Tafsir al-Jalalain* (The exegesis of the two Jalals), *7*. Beirut: Dar Ibn Khatir.

Ash-Sha'Rawi, Shaikh Mutawalli, n.d. *Tasfir ash-Shaikh Mutawalli* (Exegesis of Shaikh Mutawalli).

Bonnel, V., and Hunt, L. (Eds.). (1999). *Beyond the Cultural Turn*. Berkely, CA: University of California Press.

Bourdieu, P., and Wacquant, L.J.D. (1992.) *Réponses*. Paris. Editions du Seuil. (Transl. 1992 as *An introduction to Reflexive Sociology*, Chicago, IL: University of Chicago Press.)

Bunge, M. (1999). *T he Sociology-Philosophy Connection*. Piscataway, NJ: Transaction.

Collins, R. (1982). *Sociological Insight: an Introduction to Non-Obvious Sociology*. Oxford: Oxford University Press.

Cuche, C. (1996). *La notion de culture dans les sciences sociales.* Paris: la Découverte.

Dhaouadi, M. (1992). The Cultural Symbolic Soul: an Islamically Inspired Research Concept for the Behavioral and Social Sciences. *American Journal of Islamic Social Sciences, 9*(2), 153-172.

Dhaouadi, M. (1997). Fi-d-dalalat al-mitafiziqiya li-r-rumiz ath-thaqafiya (On the metaphysical meanings of cultural symbols). *Alam al-fikr* (The World of Thought), *25*(3), 43-49.

During, S. (Ed.). (1999). *T he Cultural Studies Reader*. (2nd ed.). London: Routledge.

Ebaugh, H.R. (2002). Return of the Sacred: Reintegrating Religion in the Social Sciences. *Social Sciences Journal for the Scientific Study of Religion, 21*(3), 385-395.

Encyclopedia of Sociology. (1974). Guilford, CT: Dushkin Publishing Group.

Fay, B. (2001). *Contemporary Philosophy of Social Sciences*. Oxford: Blackwell.

Heath, M. (2000). *Religion and New Immigration, Center for Religion and Civic Culture*. Los Angeles, CA: University of California Press.

Hunt, M. (1982). *The Universe Within*. New York: Simon and Schuster.

Ibn Khaldun. (1993). *Muqaddimah*. Beirut: Dar al-Kutub al-ilmiya, (Trans. In 1967 as The Muqaddimah: an Introduction to History. Princeton, NJ: Princeton University Press).

Long, E. (1997). *From Sociology to Cultural Studies*. Oxford: Blackwell.

Martin, B. and Rumelhard, D. (Eds.). (1999). *Cognitive Science*. (2nd ed.). San Diego, CA: Academic Press.

Parsons, T. (1966). *Societies: Evolutionary and Comparative Perspectives*. Englewood Cliffs, NJ: Prentice Hall.

Philips, D.C. (1985).*Philosophy, Science and Social Inquiry*. New York: New York Press.

Risman, B.J. and Tomaskovic-Devey, D. (Eds.). (1998). A window on the discipline, symposium. *Contemporary Sociology, 27*(1), 1-28.

Smelser, N., and Smelser, W. (1967). *Personality and Social Systems*. New York: John Wiley and Sons.

Tabara, Afif Abdulqadir al-Fattah, d. *Tafsir, juz ya sin* (Exegesis, Part ya sin (sura 36)), *23.* Beirut: Dar al-Malayin.

Wallerstein, I. (1999). The Heritage of Sociology, the Promise of Social Science. *Current Sociology, 47*(1), 1-37.

White, L. (1959). *The Evolution of Culture*. New York: McGraw Hill.

White, L., and Dillingham, A. (1973). *The Concept of Culture*. Edina, MI: Burgess International Group.

NOTE

1. The words supra-biological, super-organic and supra-organic are used by western anthropologists and sociologists to describe the cultural aspect of individuals, although in their analyses these scholars do not refer unambiguously to culture as having metaphysical features, as we demonstrate in this chapter.

Chapter Six

The Aql-Naql Theory of Human Symbols and The Making of Cultural Sociology

THE THEORY AND ITS PURPOSE

This chapter is an attempt to put forward a new cultural theory which I would like to call *the Aql-Naq l Theory of Human Symbols* (ANTHS). I label it as Aql-Naql theory, because I stress in it the combined use of both the human reasoning/Aql and the Qur'an knowledge/Naql in seeking the understanding of HS and their complex nature.

As underlined in previous chapters, ANTSH main thesis claims that humans are by nature symbolic beings before being social. This means here that the very deep central core of humans lies at a set of HS which radically distinguish them from the rest of the other living species. The theory strongly states that the system of HS occupies the very centre of the human identity which is seen, in my view, as being made of HS and the body.

Because of their assumed centrality in the human identity, HS impact on humans is expected to be of *global nature*. That is, the affects of HS on humans are not limited only to their influence on individual or collective behaviours but they are extended as well to their impact on the human bio-physiological make-up (the body).

Consequently, I think that any serious scientific analysis of human political, psychological, economic, social and cultural affairs must give first priority to the input of HS. As such, HS should be considered the crucial central basis of the making of the very distinguished human nature itself (Dhaouadi 2005: 55-66).

Thus, the (ANTHS) should also qualify to be a *transdisciplinary* general theory. The later means that it is a theory which is good to be used at the same time between and across disciplines and beyond every single discipline. Its ultimate goal is twofold: to offer a sound understanding of human affairs and to show human knowledge unity (Nicolescu 1996:66).

ANTHS AND CULTURAL SOCIOLOGY

ANTHS strongly belongs to cultural sociology and not to sociology of culture. Like cultural sociology, ANTHS considers culture an independent and central variable in the human identity and in society. It is something 'hard' and not 'soft' which has a very significant role for human individual behaviours and the social dynamics of human societies and civilizations. Thus, according the proponents of cultural sociology, social scientists must study culture within '*strong program*' and not a 'weak program' in their theoretical and empirical research (Turner 2001:137). In other words, the 'strong program' oriented sociologists consider culture an *independent variable* while culture is a dependent variable for the 'weak program' oriented sociologists (ibid:136) That is, culture must be the focus of study for the 'strong program' sociologists. This has not been so in Western sociology from its beginnings.

The pre-1960 theorists of culture like Weber, Durkheim, Marx, Parsons, Mills, Communists, Fascists and others are known to have had a `weak program` for the importance of culture in their published works.. They gave culture minor importance in their analyses (Semashko, Daloz, Erdemir 2006:831-838). Furthermore, the Birmingham School, Bourdieu, Foucault and the theory of production and consumption of culture have not done better on their part: they have adopted a `weak program` in the study of culture. All things considered, the ` weak program` trend still dominates today sociological studies of culture (Turner 2001:139) even though the `strong program` of cultural sociology is gaining more attention especially among American sociologists since the birth of the so called "cultural turn" in the late 1990s (Wolff 1999:503).

There is, however, wide consensus that American anthropologist Clifford Geertz has launched the `strong program` (SP) for the study of culture. The two axioms of the SP are: the autonomy of culture and the cultural textuality of social life. That is, culture is social life internal text.

The presentation in this chapter of the ANTHS should make it clear that I have adopted in my Aql-Naql perspective a very `strong program` in dealing with the importance of culture in the study of humans and their societies. The ANTHS may be considered an *Eastern* fair contribution to the making of both cultural sociology and the "cultural turn" which has started more than 15 years ago and has seriously challenged the meta-theoretical assumptions of many classical schools of thought.

I believe the `weak program` which most sociologists have adopted for the study of culture could be explained, in part, by what Alain Touraine considers sociologists` negligence to focus on social actors. Touraine claims that sociologists tend rather to be interested in the study of the systems like the industrial and the capitalist societies. He argues that contemporary thought has minimised the subjective side of social actors as Marx, Freud and Nietzsche had done (Wieviorka 2007: 25-27).

Without the study of the HS/ culture as a fundamental dimension of human subjectivity there can hardly be any` strong program` of sociological analysis of culture. As it will be shown in details in this chapter, the ANTHS starts its scientific explorations into the world of humans and their societies by considering first *human social actors as strong HS users by nature,* as explained in chapter I. This has required from my Aql approach a thick description of the HS system which is summarised in five new features of HS/ culture, to be explained later, of which sociologists have remained silent. As such, my perspective to the study of culture is different from most sociologists, as shown in earlier chapters. For instance, I begin the study of culture *from within*: as a distinct basic feature of human nature. On their part, sociologists study culture as external collective patterns in societies and civilizations. In other words, my approach here is made of two steps:

1. The recognition of social actors as strong HS users by nature and the need to understand the inside and outside nature of the HS system. The *thick/detailed description of HS* is, therefore, in order.
2. My Aql-oriented perspective explains the impact of HS on the dynamics of social actors and their societies.

Touraine stresses the importance for social sciences to combine the social system and the social actors in their analysis to understand and explain social action in society " it is neither excessive nor paradoxical to say that the idea of society is a major obstacle which bothers the development of social sciences because they are based on the separation and even the opposition between the system and the social actors, while the idea of society implies their direct link " (Wieviorka 2007:28).

THE MISSING INSIDE NATURE OF CULTURE

The book Cultural Sociology edited by Lyn Spillman (2007) is considered by many as the best book on the subject. For her "cultural sociology is about meaning-making .Cultural sociologists investigate how meaning-making happens"(Spillman 2007:1).The book is a Reader on cultural sociology made of papers and essays of major sociologists and anthropologists who wrote about culture. Spillman`s introduction and her notes on each paper and essay make *no mention* of the interest of the authors of the selected texts in the study of the *inside/hidden nature* of cultural elements/HS. The situation is identical in the book: The Sociology of Culture edited by Diana Crane (Crane 1995). On their part, J. Alexander and P. Smith, the two famous cultural sociologists, they hardly make any mention of the subjective, the transcendental and the spiritual dimensions of culture (Turner 2001:135-150).This is far from surprising given the marginal interest in culture among both the founders of the discipline of sociology as well as the prominent sociologists of the 20th century, as indicated before. So the general silence of sociologists on the study of the inside nature of culture (INC) is highly the expected norm. The following questions tap what I mean here by the INC: is culture a material or a spiritual part of humans? Does it have metaphysical/transcendental features? Do cultural elements have long lifespan and very strong moving force on the behaviours of the individuals and the dynamics of human societies and civilizations? The answers to such questions are dealt with in details later in the main text of my ANTHS in order to underline a profile of the inside anatomy of the HS system/culture.

The lack of the study of the INC is true of Spillman's comments on some very famous scholars in the landscape of culture like Benedict, Shils, Geertz and Bourdieu. None of them and other cited authors in the book has given first priority to the study of the INC. Their focus has been rather on *external side of culture*. The same thing is also true of the content of the book: The Sociology of Culture edited by Crane and in the chapter of Smith and Alexander (Turner 2001:135-150). This is in consistency with the spirit as well as with the methodology of Positivism which was strongly advocated by the founder of Western sociology, August Comte.

As referred to before, few basic books on culture are also witness of silence on the INC. The Concept of Culture (White1973), Culture(Kuper 1999), La notion de culture dans les sciences sociales (Cuche 1996) hardly speak about the INC let alone analyze it and discuss it.This is no surprise when we know that some anthropologists , as seen the last chapter, have often a vague idea about what culture is .Ralph Linton asks "is culture real?" or "Does it exist?(White 1973) For Radcliffe-Brown culture is a word that designates no concrete reality but only an abstraction, and a very vague abstraction at that. M.E Spiro takes similar position on culture (White 1973:26).

The legitimate question now is this: how could sociologists and social scientists in general study culture in a meaningful way in society and be able to make sound interpretations of cultures or come to solid insights on the meaning-making process without having first a strong understanding of the INC per se and its impact on social actors' actions?

As mentioned before, the domination of the Positivist perspective and that of Behaviorism should help explain the great reservations and skepticism manifested by the social scientists with regard to the inside dimensions of culture and, subsequently, to its deep latent/hidden nature. The heavy impact of the exclusion or the marginalization of the recognition and, thus, the study and understanding of the INC has led, on the one hand, to *a later coming* of both sociology of culture and of cultural sociology and, on the other hand, to a rather *wide weakness* in many predictions, theories and paradigms of contemporary social sciences. The increasing interest especially by American sociologists in these two types of sociology may promote the credibility of today discipline of sociology in the West and, consequently, in the East.

WHAT IS A THEORY?

There are many definitions of the word `theory` in social sciences. One definition considers a theory a set of concepts and propositions which aim to *explain* a given phenomenon (Dortier 2004:812).Another definition sees a social theory as any attempt to explain facets of social life (Encyclopaedia of Sociology 1973:274). For hard sciences, "a theory is a general principle supported by a substantial body of scientific evidence which explains observed facts…a theory offers an intellectual framework for future discussion, investigation and refinement" (Bothamley 1993:523)

As to the scientific stand of sociological theories, J.Turner saw an increasing cynicism about the prospects of the emergence of scientific sociological theories during the last decade of 20th century. This was very different around sixty years ago when there was real and great optimism that sociology would sit at the table of scientists. But today, there is much smaller number of sociological theorists who hold such a position (Turner 2001:30.).This attitude on the part of some sociologists is *an anti-science attitude*. The spirit of real and serious science should not ethically make discrimination against the progress of science in one field and advocate its progress in another. Thus, sociologists and other social scientists can really join the ranks of their fellow hardcore scientists if they improve their scientific research toolkit in studying the phenomena in their fields. This would allow them to build credible theories which can explain individual behaviours as well as the social dynamics of human societies and civilizations.

The negative view toward the scientific stand of the discipline of sociology is not limited to sociologists themselves. Hardcore scientists have also a more negative perception of the scientific stand of social sciences at large. In 2000 the journal New Scientist published an editorial on Creationism and

Evolution which *rules out any hope for social sciences* to have a credible scientific knowledge on the phenomena they study. The editorial asks:" Will it (science) tell us how to behave towards our fellow humans?" The answer of the editorial is squarely negative. For the author of the editorial, science is simply the wrong tool to answer this question and similar ones. In such an attitude, there is an obvious *narrow view* of the nature of science. In a time of globalisation, identity crises, environmental concerns, worldwide fears of modern science hard and software destructive products…how much respect should be accorded to science which does not believe, based on its false view of things, that we humans can in fact establish reliable scientific understanding and explanation of human phenomena?

Such a position on the part of hardcore scientists and soft (social) scientists displays an extreme unsuitable view of the real horizons of science. This is terribly unacceptable in our time which has been witnessing among scientists and scholars a growing trend in favour of cooperation between disciplines (interdisciplinarity) studying phenomena as complex entities with new scientific paradigms which advocate that scientists, researchers, scholars…should be open minded to all types of insights which serve them well in establishing credible and coherent scientific knowledge (Wilson 1999).

BASIC OBSERVATIONS AND THE MAKING OF THE ANTHS

My new ANTHS is exclusively founded on my personal thinking reason/Aql. It exists neither in my book (*Toward Islamic Sociology of Cultural Symbols 1996*) nor in the literature of social sciences I am familiar with so far. The new ANTHS is based on a set of five observations/concepts of my own:

1. The process of the human body growth and maturation is very slow compared with those of other living beings. For instance, on average humans begin walking at the age of one year, while animals may walk within few hours or days after their birth.
2. In general, humans have longe*r* lifespan than those of most of the other species.
3. The human race has a dominant role in the administration, management and control of this world.
4. Humans are privileged by what we have called earlier *HS* system: spoken and written language, thought, religion, knowledge/science, laws, myths, cultural values and norms…
5. In the perspective of my theory (the ANTHS), the human identity is made up of two parts: the body and HS. As such, it is fully a dualistic identity which is often referred to in religion and philosophy as an identity made of body and soul.

I sent an e-mail message to the Scientific American (SA) journal asking specifically for an explanation of the slow growth and maturation of the human body. The SA editor has remained silent for about a year. I received the reply message, October 19, 2005, which had no answer to our question. The SA editor's message advised me only to search for possible answers to my question in anthropology's websites.

POTENTIAL EXPLANATION OF MY THEORY

In the absence of SA scientific explanation to the human body slow growth phenomenon, I found myself as a researcher compelled to look for a potential explanatory hypothesis of ANTHS: the slow human body growth and maturation could be accounted for by the assumption which sees that human global growth and maturation involve *two fronts*: The body front and that of HS. In short, the growth and maturation of non-human species are uni-dimensional (body) because of their lack of HS in the most complex human sense of the term. In contrast, the growth and maturation of humans are bi-dimensional. That is, they involve two levels: the body level and the HS level. So, the process of two levels is considered, in my hypothesis of the ANTHS, to be behind the human slow body growth and maturation. This assumption is based on logical reasoning. Logical reasoning would conclude that the rapid body growth and maturation among the non-humans is assumed to be due to the uni-dimensional/body process of growth and maturation .While the slow body growth and maturation among humans is due to the fact that they go through *two processes* of growth and maturation. In logical reasoning terms, it takes longer time for the accomplishment of the two processes of growth and maturation to materialise than for just one single process. That is, the process of human body growth and maturation is slowed down, so to speak, among humans because humans are involved in *a second process* of growth and maturation represented by HS. Furthermore, the growth and maturation of HS appear to be by their own nature slower than the human body processes of growth and maturation. While the latter reach their peak of growth and maturation in the twenties (Rischer, Easton 1992:423), some features of HS reach their higher and highest stages of growth and maturation much later in human lifespan. For instance, humans could hardly reach, before the age of 40 years, the peak of growth and maturation in the fields of thought, religious experience and knowledge and science. This gives strong legitimacy to humans' strong need for longer lifespan as shown in drawing I below. In other words, the human longer lifespan could be seen as the outcome of two factors:

1. The slow human pace of body growth and maturation and

2. The apparent innate tendency of HS to grow and mature slowly.

The human body growth and maturation peak in the twenties helps explain also two features of human life: 1- athletes are known to often retire after they reach the age of 25 years or so .2- on the intellectual/thought level, humans can hardly manifest mature thinking before the twenties. This could be explained as follows: once humans have, so to speak, finished the business of their body growth and maturation in the twenties, they can then *concentrate* more on the development and maturation of their HS for the rest of their lives. This should explain as well why real high mature scientific theories and intellectual complex thought can not usually see the light before the age of 40 years.

This gives legitimacy to my theory which stipulates that humans are by nature cultural symbolic beings. In other words, HS are at the core of the human race's identity, because they strongly influence/determine the remaining four distinctive human features (1, 2, 3, 5) as shown in the drawing of chapter I. This makes the ANTHS a *very 'strong program'* culture oriented theory. Since HS /culture are very central to its epistemology, its explanatory perspective and its theorizing about the behaviours of human individuals and the social dynamics of human societies. The ANTHS should, thus, qualify to be an avant-garde theory for today emerging cultural sociology (Spillman 2007). As elaborated, the ANTHS is *fully new* in its conceptualization, its theorizing vision and in its understanding and explanation of human phenomena.

CULTURAL SOCIOLOGY AS A CORE DISCIPLINE

Having established, through the Aql/human reason analysis here and in previous chapters, that HS are very central to human identity and are also very distinctive of the human race, *HS* should, thus, be considered as *first class source/ reference* for social scientists whose studies attempt to understand and explain the behaviours of individuals as well as the social dynamics of human societies and civilizations. There is, therefore, a strong legitimacy for cultural sociology to be established, promoted and defended by sociologists. Because this discipline strongly uses the basic human foundations (HS) for the understanding of human behaviours and societies' dynamics. Unlike other branches of sociology which often deal with peripheral issues in dealing with humans and their societies, cultural sociology addresses and focuses its attention deeply on those most fundamental elements (HS) without which neither humans nor their own societies could come into existence as we know them as distinct and leading features in this world. Based on this, cultural sociology is strongly qualified to be seen as *the top discipline* not only in the field of sociology but in all other fields of social sciences.

THE QU RAN'S CULTURAL 'STRONG PROGRAM'

So far, I have elaborated my own Aql/human reasoning research into the making of the ANTHS. Turn now to the use of the Naql/the Qur'an in order to articulate the Aql-Naql synthesis of the ANTHS. As shown in the above sections of this chapter, my Aql approach strongly belongs to cultural sociology which considers *HS/culture an independent variable.* As outlined in previous chapters, the classical period (pre-1960) of sociologists is seen by J. Alexander as the period of 'weak program' in the social theory of culture. This period includes "the sociologies of Weber, Durkheim, Marx, Mills and others as well as Communists and Fascists" (Semashko 2006: 836). Alexander believes the 'weak program' still dominates the modern (post- 1960) period as manifested in the works of the Birmingham School, Bourdieu, Foucault and the theory of 'the production and consumption of culture' (ibid). As mentioned before, American anthropologist Clifford Geertz has changed the place of culture in the perspectives of modern social sciences (Geertz 1964). For him, culture has its autonomy and human societies are similar to texts where the reading of their meanings is very central. Alexander believes that the recognition of the autonomy of culture by cultural sociologists is *'the single most important quality of a strong program'* (Alexander 2003:13).

My already presented Aql analysis of HS centrality in the human identity and Geertz`s are also endorsed by *the Islamic perspective* found in the *Qur'an/the Naql.* Inside and insightful reading and interpretation of the text of the Qur'an lead to the discovery that the Muslim Holy Book has indeed a cultural `strong program`. That is, *it considers humans as profoundly HS beings*: cultural symbolic beings.

In order to identify the nature of HS / culture as well as their importance in the identity of the human agent in the Qur'an outlook, I found no better reference than the Qur'an itself which is Islam's first authoritative reference text. There are many verses in it that speak with clarity of human nature. I have chosen in this chapter only two verses which do describe in full the basic components of human nature. The two verses in question are: Behold! Thy Lord said to the angels: 1 am about to create man, from sounding clay from mud moulded into shape. When 1 have fashioned him (in due proportion) and breathed into him of *My spirit,* fall ye down in obeisance unto him (The Qur'an 15: 28-29). *Human nature,* according to these two verses, is *dualistic* in nature. It is made up of *clay* and the *divine breathed spirit.*

As to which one of these two components is more important in the making of human nature and, thus, human identity, one good inside and logical
interpretation of these two verses allows one to assert that the Qur'an gives
more importance to the side of the divine breathed spirit into the human
entity. Since the angels were ordered by God to prostrate to Adam immediately after, and *not before*, the divine spirit was breathed into him. The
angels' prostrating act before Adam is seen as a symbolic sign of respect to
this godly new privileged creature who has been the only creature to receive
a special divine breathed spirit. The position of the Qur'an in favour of the
spiritual dimension of human nature is a fundamental permanent principle
which runs throughout the entire text of the Qur'an. We are told again and
again in the verses of the 114 Surahs/ chapters of the Qur'an, that human
individuals, groups, communities, societies and civilizations can achieve excellence only when their divine breathed spirit *dominates* the materialistic
(clay) side of their human nature.

The interpretation of the meaning of the verses of the Qur'an has been a
major concern for Muslims in the past and in the present. I have selected a
very limited sample of the exegitists (al-Mufassirun) of the Qur'an who have
done their work either in Arabic or in English. Fakhrudine al-Razi who died
in 1210 and Ahmad al-Ansari al-Qurtubi who died around 1293 are two well
known exegitists of the Qur'an of past Muslim civilization. There are also
two widely used interpretations of the Qur'an which are written in Arabic in
the last century by Said Qutb and Muhammad Tahar Ben Achour. In English,
there are today two famous interpretations of the Qur'an. Each one of them is
considered a highly credible reference by English speaking Muslims. Yusuf
Ali and Muhammad Assad are the authors of the two English Qur'anic trans-
lations.

AI-Razi (AL-Razi (1981:185-86) interpreted the word spirit (ruh) as wind
which can be breathed in. Then, he admits that real knowledge of the divine
spirit is not accessible to humans. As to al-Qurtubi's (Al-Qurtubi 1967; 24-
25) interpretation of the word spirit, it is not very different from al-Razi's
.For him, the spirit is like a wind and it has a gentile entity. As to the two
contemporary Arab exegetists of the Qur'an, Said Qutb (Qutub 1985:35, 39)
speaks of the divine spirit as that breath which has enabled the human race to
transcend its material (clay) make up and reach out for the spiritual horizon
where hearts and minds are in action. On his part, Ben Achour (Ben Achour:
no date 43-47), sees in the divine breath into Adam as a symbol of man's
greatness in the eyes of God. Yusuf Ali gives the following meaning to God's
breathed spirit into man: the breathing of Allah's spirit into man, i.e., the
faculty of God-like knowledge and will which, if rightly used, would give
man superiority over other creatures (Ali 1989:625). As to Muhammad Assad, he interprets the divine spirit this way:" God's "breathing of His spirit"

into man is obviously a metaphor for His endowing him with life and consciousness: that is, with a soul". (Assad 1980:386).

These six interpretations of the word "spirit" are generally *vague* as to the specific nature of the breathed divine spirit into man. Yusuf Ali's interpretation of the word ruh/spirit is perhaps the most tangible of all interpretations referred to here. As mentioned before, the word spirit meant for him God-like knowledge and will which were given only to man. It is an interpretation which attempts to avoid to be entangled into the vagueness and generality reflected in the other interpretations.1n other words, his interpretation of the breathed divine spirit as *"God-like, knowledge and will'* invested in man could constitute one step toward helping identifying more concretely the specific identity of the very nature of the breathed divine spirit into man.

This would require that `the divine breathed spirit` be operationalized in social sciences terminology. The term '*operational* is used in modern social sciences to mean that social scientists should attempt to make vague phenomena and ideas more tangible. That is, quantifiable and measurable if possible. So the vague phenomena and ideas in question become operational and empirically manageable. The process of making things operational is certainly inspired by the epistemology of Western modern science and knowledge. This epistemology relies heavily in its understanding and explanation of phenomena on identifiable, quantitative and measurable variables and causes. The degree of success in this process varies from one category of phenomena to the other. For instance, the so called subjective phenomena (personal feelings, opinions etc.) are less easy to make operational than the objective phenomena out there in the external world. Nonetheless, efforts must be made to identify as concretely as possible the hidden dimensions of vague phenomena. As pointed out earlier, the meaning of the divine spirit as conveyed by the six exegetists of the two verses of the Qur'an remains rather vague. There is a need, therefore, to develop some sort of *methodology* that helps avoid the use of vague and general labels which are of no help for a closer and a more tangible understanding of the nature of the breathed divine spirit. In order to dissipate the obscurity surrounding the nature of the breathed divine spirit, I need to adopt the following methodology. First, I should identify objectively and in tangible terms those elements which really distinguish humans from the rest of the other species and make them superior over all of them. As mentioned in other previous chapters, HS (language, thought, beliefs, science/knowledge, cultural norms and values, laws etc.) are what distinguish humans from the rest of the species. The two verses of the Qur'an referred to here speak also explicitly of man's distinct and prestigious status among all other creatures including the angels themselves who were asked by God to prostrate to Adam. *The breathed divine spirit* appears to be behind the special place which was accorded to the human race on this planet. As indicated before, God order to the angels to prostrate to Adam came immediately after and not before the event of the divine breath took place into Adam.

Thus, the human objective reasoning analysis (the Aql) and the Qur'an revealed text (the Naql) *concur on the human superiority over the other species*. While the former relates it to the human race's unique HS, the latter explains the humans' distinct status by the breathed divine spirit (ruh) into them. Thus, *there is a strong agreement between the two perspectives*. The Qur'an consistently attributes humankind distinct superiority over the other living species to its HS/culture as manifested in language use, science, thinking, learning, religion, laws, norms, moral ethics etc… In other words, both approaches point to the crucial role of HS in the making of human superiority/distinctiveness.

However, in the Qur'an perspective, the divine breathed spirit as a source of man's superiority/distinctiveness may have a broader meaning than the HS per se. That is, the broader meaning would cover everything that distinguishes humans from the non-humans. The drawing below shows the kind of overlapping which exists between HS and the divine breathed spirit as the two determining factors of the superiority/distinctiveness of the human race. It remains to be emphasized here that HS are the key tangible factor in the divine breathed spirit which offers the human race an overwhelming domination over the rest of the species in the world.

My operational analysis of HS has so far clarified the broader nature of the divine breathed spirit. In my interpretation, the latter must, at least, include the human HS. In other words, the divine breathed spirit must include the human HS themselves or more than that. With this, the identity of the divine breathed spirit is no longer as obscure as it was in the six interpretations of the Qur'an's exegetists outlined above. So, in these two Qur'an verses the word 'ruh' must first mean HS. This implies that HS divine nature can explain *the potential eternity* of human thought of philosophers, social thinkers, scientists… referred to earlier. Because human thought is part of HS in my Aql-conceptualization. I also saw that it has a metaphysical divine origin according to the Qur'an outlook as just outlined. So, it is strongly eligible for long lifespan or even eternity.

All things considered, I see eye to eye with Professor Zaglul Annajar who argues that the Qur'an exegetists need credible modern scientific knowledge to convey the right meanings of the Qur'an verses for both natural and social sciences (Annajar 2002).

The above interpretation of the two verses makes it clear that the text of the Qur'an has a *very cultural ` strong program`*. Since the human unique mastership in the world comes from the breathed divine spirit/HS/culture. That is, HS are so central in the identity of the human agents and are independent variables. Their global impact on the human biology, as shown from chapter I and after, the behaviors of individuals and the dynamics of human

The Origin of Human Superiority/Distinctiveness

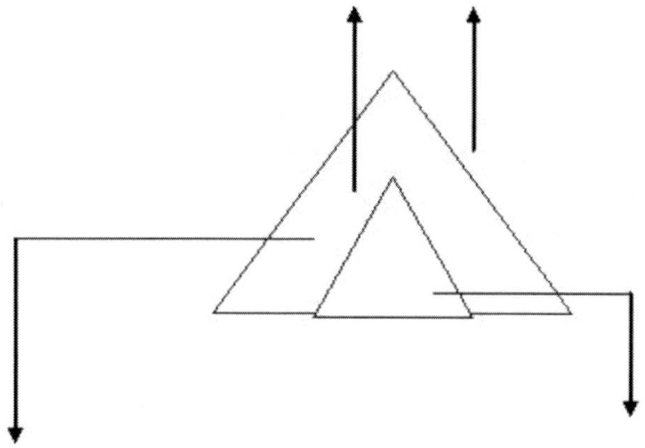

The Entire Breathed

Divine Spirit/EBDS

HS

Part of EBDS or all of it

Figure 6.1.

societies and civilizations is very great. This gives strong legitimacy to the much needed pressing work on cultural sociology. This should bring about *serious reform* in the discipline of sociology that has neglected for so long the fundamental role of culture as independent variable in the making of sociology as a rigorous and scientific system of knowledge of credible understanding and explanation of phenomena through the use of valid methodology and sociological theory.

The use in this chapter of the human analytical reasoning/the Aql and the Qur'an verses/the Naql show that HS are central to the identities of the human agents. *The Muslim classical learned mind* combines both use of human reasoning/the Aql and revelation /the Naql in its efforts to create and establish trustworthy knowledge and science. From the Islamic perspective, *the Aql-Naql mind* is an *ideal type mind* as far as securing credible and exhaustive knowledge and science particularly in the ethics and moral values and norms of cultures of human societies and civilizations. Ibn Khaldun is a good example who fully used the Aql-Naql mind in his famous work of The Muqaddimah (Dhaouadi 2005: 585-591).

CONCLUSION

The thesis of the theory (the ANTHS) in this chapter offers a number of novelties in the social sciences. It strongly argues that humans are profoundly *homo symbolicus:* great users of human symbols (HS). This is rarely underlined in modern social sciences which often use other terms to describe man like homo sociologicus, homo oeconomicus and homo politicus. I stress that this shortcoming undermines the credibility of those sciences in the making of well grounded concepts and theories. There is also a transparent novelty both in my Aql/human reasoning conceptualization and my Naql interpretation of HS in the included drawing. These new insights on the nature of HS in the Aql-Naql perspectives have led to the birth and may be to the good standing of the ANTHS. As such, the ANTHS highly qualifies to be *a cultural theory* that can explain various different human phenomena from the slow human body growth and maturation to the dialogue/clash of human cultures/civilizations to be presented and discussed in the last chapter of this book. The synthesis of the Aql-Naql approaches lends support to the idea of the Islamisation of knowledge which ultimately means finding reliable correspondence/matching between the findings of human reasoning analysis /Aql and those of the divine revealed Naql sources.

ANTHS' extreme emphasis on the centrality of HS in the human identity and, consequently, on their impact on human action in single and collective human affairs make ANTHS very legitimate for the discipline of cultural sociology. The latter considers culture *an independent variable* of great weight and influence on individual and social human affairs. As such, the framework of the ANTHS can only enhance and promote the chance for the solid growing and development of cultural sociology.

REFERENCES

Alexander, J. (Ed.). (2003). *The Meanings of Social Life: A Cultural Sociology*. Oxford, New York: Oxford University Press.

Al-Qurtubi, A.A. (1967). *Al Jamaa li Ahkam al Quran* (in Arabic). Cairo, Dar al Kitab al Arabi, X.

Al-Razi, F. (1981). *Tafsiru al Quran* (in Arabic). Beirut, Dar el Fikr, X.

Annajar, Z. (2002). *The Scientific Immitability of the Quran , Part I.* (3rd ed.). Cairo: Shorouk International Library.

Assad, M. (1980). *The Message of the Quran*. Gibraltar: Dar al Andalus.

Ben Achour, M.T. (no date). *Tafsir al Tahrir wa al Tanwir* (in Arabic). Tunis: Edition Maison Tunisienne.

Bochner, S. (Ed.). (1985). *Culture in Contact*. Oxford, New York: Pergamon Press.

Bothamley, J. (1993). *Dictionary of Theories*. London: Gale Research International Ltd.

Calvet, L-J. (1987). *La guerre des langues et les politiques linguistiques*. Paris: Payot.

Crane, D. (1995). *The Sociology of Culture*. Oxford: Basil Blackwell Ltd.

Cuche, D. (1996). *La notion de la culture dans les sciences sociales*. Paris: La Decouverte.

Khaldun, Ibn. (1974). *The Muqaddimah: An Introduction to History*. Dawood, N.J. (Ed.). (Franz Rosenthal, Trans.). Princeton Bolling Series: Princeton University Press.

Dhaouadi, M. (2006). *Culture in the Social Science and the Islamic Perspectives* (in Arabic). Beirut: Dar al Kitab al Jadid Ltd.

Dhaouadi, M. (2005). The Ibar: Lessons of Ibn Khaldun's Umran Mind. *Contemporary Sociology, 34*(6), 585-591.

Dhaouadi, M. (2005). The West's difficulties for dialogue with the Arab Muslim World (in Arabic). *Hewar Al Arab*, 8-15.

Dhaouadi, M. (2005). New perspective on human nature (in Arabic). Al Thaqafa al Nafsia al Mutakhassissa (specializad Psychological Journal), *62*, 55-66.

Dhaouadi, M. (2005). The ABC of cultural symbols: for a more accurate understanding of important issues in today's world (in Arabic). *Al Adab Journal, 53*, 5-12.

Dhaouadi , M. (2003-2004). An Investigation into the Determinants of Ibn Khaldun's Umran Mind. *Annals of The Arts and Social Sciences*. The Academic Publication Council, Kuwait University, Monograph 208, *24*.

Dhaouadi, M. (1990). Ibn Khaldun: the Founding Father of Eastern Sociology. *International Sociology*. *5*(3), 319-335.

Dhaouadi, M. (1997). *New Explorations Into the Making of Ibn Khaldun's Umran Mind*. Kuala Lumpur: A.S. Noordeen

Encyclopedia of Sociology. (1973). Guilford: The Dushkin Publishing Group Inc.

Dortier, J-F. (2004). *Le dictionnaire des sciences humaines*. Auxerelle Cedex: Editions Sciences Humaines.

Dortier, J-F. (2005-2006). L'origine des cultures. *Les Grands Dossiers des Sciences Humaines, 1*.

Elmessiri, A.W. (Ed.). (2006). *Epistemological Bias in the Physical and Social Sciences*. London, Washington: The International Institute of Islamic Thought.

Geertz, C. (1964). *The Interpretation of Cultures*. New York: Basic Books.

Huntington, S. (Dec. 2001-Feb. 2002). *Newsweek* Special Davos Edition, 9.

Huntington, S. (1993). The Clash of Civilizations. *Foreign Affairs, 72*. Excerpts in the book: *The Globalization Reader* edited by F. Lechner and J. Boli. Malden/USA.

Kuper, A. (1999). *Culture: The Anthropologists' Account*. Cambridge, MA: Harvard University Press.

Nicolescu, B. (1996). *La transdisciplinarité*. Manifeste, Paris: Editions Du Rocher.

Pedler, K. (1981). *Mind Over Matter*. London: Thames Methuen.

Qutb, S. (1985). *Zilal al Qur'an* (in Arabic). Beirut: Dar al Sharq .

Rischer, C., Easton, T. (1992). *Focus on Human Biology*. New York: Harper Collins Publishers.

Saadi, M. (2006). *The Future of International Relations: From the Clash of Civilizations to the Humanization of Civilization and the Culture of Peace* (in Arabic). Beirut: Centre for Arab Unity Studies

Semashko, L. and others. (2006). *International Sociology Review of Book s, 2*(6), 829-38.

Shahine, A.S. (1997). *The Avoidence of Contradicion Between Reason and Revelation in Ibn Taymiyya's Thought (*in Arabic). Cairo: Al Ahram Center for Translation and Publications

Snow, C.P. (1963). *The Two Cultures: And a Second Look*. New York: Cambridge University Press

Spillman, L. (2002). *Cultural Sociology*. Oxford: Blackwell Publishing Ltd.

Toynbee, A. (1956). *The Study of History*. London, UK: Oxford University Press.

Turner, J.H (2001). *Handbook of Sociological Theory*. New York: Kluwer Academic/Plenum Publishers.

White, L. (1973). *The Concept of Culture*. Edina, MN:Alpha Editions.

Wieviorka, M. (2007). *Les sciences sociales en mutation*. Auxerre Cedex: Editions Sciences Humaines.

Wilson, E. (1999). *Consilience: The Unity of Knowledge*. New York: Vintage Books.

Wilson, E. (1975). *Sociobiology: The New Synthesis*. Cambridge, MA: Harvard University Press.

Wolff, J. (1999). Cultural Studies and the Sociology of Culture. *Contemporary Sociology ,* 28(5), 499-506.
Yusuf, A. (1989). *The Holy Quran : Text, Translation and Commentary.* Anna Corporation, Brentwood, Maryland, USA.

III

Three Case Studies within the HS Perspective

Chapter Seven

HS Behind Human Longer Lifespan

INTRODUCTION

In this chapter, I use HS as an interdisciplinary concept. As outlined in previous chapters, HS refer to chosen traits which distinguish radically the human species from the rest of the other living species. As stressed before, spoken and written language, thought, religion, knowledge/science, laws, myths, cultural values and norms… are specific human characteristics. With them only has come the very legitimacy of the domination of the human race over the other species. As such, HS constitute the most fundamental distinct basis of the human identity. It has already been shown that the impact of HS on humans ought to be remarkable and broadly extensive. That is, their influence on humans is assumed to be wide ranging. They affect various dimensions of the human social actors. I argue more extensively in this chapter that HS have bearing not only on the social, cultural and psychological aspects of humans, but also on their biology. This strongly justifies claim that humans are first of all culture-symbolic beings by nature. Looking at HS this way and shedding insights on the credibility of those assumptions will make the HS set a credible interdisciplinary concept. In this chapter, I limit my use of HS manly to the disciplines of biology, social sciences and human sciences.

HS AND THEIR CRUCIAL USE IN SOFT AND HARD SCIENCES

My main thesis in this chapter would like to strongly argue that the study of the behaviours of human individuals and the dynamics of their societies must give priority to what distinguishes them most from other living beings and their collectivities. As stressed in this book, I consider HS as the crucial divide between the human species and the rest of the other species. In my view, HS constitute the most central and fundamental part of individual and collective human identities. In other words, HS are the very core of the human species. On the one hand, other known living species could compete neither quantitatively nor qualitatively with the human species on the HS scale. In short, HS are the privilege of the humans and their communities. On the other hand, without HS the Homo sapiens can not alone claim leadership and domination in this world/universe as underlined in chapter I of Part I of the book in particular. As such, HS are second to none in the determination of the human's supremacy over the other species. So, they are indeed the ultimate center of humans as a distinguished special species. The first class centrality of HS in the making of human individuals and communities makes its impact in human affaires very compelling. That is, I can hardly imagine human social action of social actors and their collectivities without HS input. At one level, HS are often the direct micro and macro- motivating forces of social action in social life. At another level, HS play a screening role for both inside the social actor's personality and the outside environment's potential influential factors to which human communities and their members are exposed. In other terms, HS represent a sort of a filter to the influential forces that orient and ultimately shape human social action. They are, so to speak, the checking board that determines the particular kind of social action which individuals and collectivities find themselves engaged in. My assumptions on the nature of HS (their first class position in the identity making of humans and their communities and their weightful impact on human social action) lead me, consequently, to take a critical stand of those social science whose analytical perspectives give rather priority to the economico-socio-structural and biological (Sociobiology) factors as capital determining forces of social action. In their explanations of individuals' behaviours and societies's dynamics Marxists emphasize the determining role of economic factors, functionalist sociologists stress the socio-structures of collectivities and sociobiologists give great importance to biological parameters . While social scientists must give credit to all these factors in their analysis of individual as well as collective behaviours, they should not, however, conceive the impact of the bio-economico-socio-structural variables'automatic unilinear irresistible ones like the impact of instinctual drives on behaviours among animals. There is an overwhelming evidence from contemporary social sciences that the differences in behaviours among individuals within the same community or belonging to various societies are largely due to cultural differences. That is, human behaviour is strongly culturally determined'. This is not true only of biological factors but also of their socio-structuro-economic counterparts. The impact of HS on the individuals' behaviours and their collectivities are systematically cross-checked through their own cultural systems which often play the role of a vigilant referee. As such, in the final analysis the impact of

HS on the human social action is very compelling indeed. With this extreme importance of HS in mind, they must become the first reference framework of social scientists for both comprehension and explanation of human behaviour and the community's dynamics .The current strong emergence of both Cognitive Psychology (Bly, Rumechatt 1999) as the leading subdivision in the field of psychology and of Sociology of Culture or Cultural Sociology (Bonnell, Hunt 1999, Crane 1995, Spillman 2007) as also a front line growing subdiscipline of sociology is a strong indicator that the role of HS in the analysis of society's dynamics and the individuals' behaviours is increasingly getting widely recognized in the social sciences. This change of perspective is quite legitimate because of the central role HS play in the making of human affairs, as emphasized in this book. Thus, it is hardly an exaggeration to expect other branches of social sciences to give more attention to the impact of the crucial parameters of HS in their attempts to comprehend and explain the behaviours of human agencies as well as the dynamics of human collectivities. The rather imposing impact of HS on the orientation as well as the ultimate determination of human social action, is not only limited to its comprehension and explanation both in the micro and macro senses. My conceptualization of HS constitutes also a conceptual framework. That is, an intellectual vision of the human world where HS are considered the most central components of the human identity. As pointed out in the first chapter of this book, HS could become a strong potential social science framework for social theory building about the behaviours of social actors and the collective social action of human communities. As defined, a social theory is an intellectual perspective that can explain aspects/phenomena of social life (Baert 1988: 1). In other words, HS could empower social science researchers to actively engage in theory building at the micro and macro levels of human social life. Since humans and their collectities are perceived in this book's thesis as profoundly culturally oriented (HS) by nature, there is hardly any surprise to consider HS as a general resourceful kit for wide legitimate and credible theory building about human societies and their members.

As such, I consider HS an interdisciplinary masterpiece concept for the social and human sciences. But its great importance is hardy limited to these soft sciences. I have found also, as shown in chapter I of this work that hard/natural sciences could benefit considerably from my concept of HS in their understanding and explanation of biological phenomena. The latter are the focus of this chapter. I use the concept of HS to examine a very unusual biological case study which has not been known to have been addressed and analysed both by hard sciences as well as by soft sciences. As an interdisciplinary concept, HS are used here to help explain their determining impact on the longer human lifespan[1] .

THE PHENOMENON UNDER STUDY AND ITS METHODOLOGY

The phenomenon studied in this chapter and its thesis are inspired neither by my readings in modern Western social sciences and other related disciplines in English, French and Arabic nor by my Western and Eastern academic and scholarly contacts with colleagues in universities, research centers, intellectual seminars and conferences.

Actually, *I was shocked* when the idea of the correlation between HS and longer human lifespan began in 1995 to assert gradually itself in my thinking. I asked my self: how come I have not seen any reference for this correlation in all the written materials I have come across in social sciences and in other disciplines? I had a strange feeling. But my discomfort was lessened somewhat following talking to colleagues and students about that correlation. Practically, all of them have also expressed their *dismay and amazement* that they themselves have not thought of this relationship between human HS and the longer lifespan of the human species.

As such, one can hardly hope to find modern literature in the different fields of sciences on this subject matter .I even had difficulty to have an easy access to information about the average lifespan of the members of other living species. Such information is certainly important for the investigation of the relationship between HS and the lifespan of living species. I decided to write to the National Geographic Society as well as to Discover magazine in the USA asking them if they have ever published studies, articles and books on the longevity of animals. I received no answer from Discover magazine. But, the editor of the National Geographic Society has written back to me (Feb. 23, 95) saying: "I have not published an article on the longevity of animals nor was 1 able to find a book on the subject in our library. However, 1 did find the enclosed chart in the World Almanac and Books of Facts 1994 that might be of some help".

It is against this background that I was led to take two contradictory positions: (1) I thought that my idea about the correlation between HS and longer human lifespan is completely an ill-founded idea. This is why there has been no mention of it anywhere or (2) I thought that the idea of this correlation is really *a new one*. So it deserves to be explored in full in order to evaluate its credibility. I chose option (2) in spite of the enormous scientific challenges and risks involved for the lonely researcher.

Common people's observations as well as those of scientists concur that members of the human species live, on the average, *longer life* than most of the members of the animal species. Therefore, it is legitimate to ask why is there this difference? I attempt to answer this question through basic facts and observations of two perspectives. The first perspective relies heavily on modern bio-genetic science. As to the second perspective, it draws its explanation from my HS framework. As briefly explained in chapter I of this book, HS are determinant factors for both the slow growth of the human body as well as the longer human lifespan. The latter will be analyzed at the end of this chapter by religious and philosophical perspectives. This approach is compatible with the interdisciplinary framework adopted in this work[2] .

THE HUMAN SPECIES' LONGER LIFESPAN

I need here to take a look at the average age differences between the members of the human species, and those of a limited sample of animals. The average lifespan in years of certain animals are as follows: lions (15), tigers (16), sheep (12), cows (15), pigs (10), rabbits (5), gorilla (20), horses (20), elephants (40)(4). But the average of the lifespan of humans is significantly longer than the average lifespan of the animals referred to here. Even before the modern medical scientific revolution, the average human lifespan in some human societies was around 40 years or more.

THE BIOGENETIC PERSPECTIVE ON THE HUMAN LIFESPAN

The modern bio-genetic science is inclined to explain the longer human lifespan by the bio-genetic factor in the human species make-up. Scientific research continues to underline the crucial importance which the genes play on numerous aspects of the human identity and behaviour. In the four last decades or so some scientists have even explained the social behaviour of humans through facts and information gathered by the science of biology and genetics. The new sub-discipline of Sociobiology is an example. Sociobiologists explain a number of human social behaviours like suicide and forbidden marriage between sisters and brothers by the deterministic logic of the human biology and genes. Likewise, Geneticists view that the individual's lifespan is strongly determined by the kind of genes he/she has.

On the one hand, they consider that the age of 120 years is somewhat the maximum age human beings could reach. In other words, the inherent make-up of genes of the members of the human race allow them to reach the age of 120 years. In contrast to this, the genes of the animal species do not permit their members to reach that very long age. It is, therefore, the type of genes which each living species has that ultimately determines the maximum number of years which certain members of given species could live. Modern scientific evidence strongly shows that the human type of genes plays a crucial role in the making of the longer human lifespan. Much was written in magazines and newspapers about the world's oldest French lady: Jeanne Calment who was 120 years old. The late French president, François Miitterand, had given her a diploma for being the oldest known human individual in the world. Scientists have found out that reaching very old age appears to run into families. Mrs Calment's mother died at the age of 86 years while her father lived longer than her mother. He died when he was 93 years old. Thus, it is through the working of the genes that old age could become a hereditary phenomenon among humans. Scientists believe that individuals who live very long may have a type of genes which has a special resistance against the harmful impact of the chemical remains which result from the nutrition process in the human body. These chemical residues are assumed to damage more seriously the DNA of the majority of the population as it grows older. This scientific observation implies that the human race may have *a better immune system* than other living species in dealing with the chemical remains mentioned before. However, this observation may offer just an apparent explanation to what may make humans enjoy longer lifespan. In order for such an explanation to have a stronger credibility, it needs to explain also why the better immune system of the genes has largely been confined to the human race. I don't know at this time if the sciences of biology and genetics have their own scientific explanation for this human peculiarity. I e-mailed in 2004 the Scientific American (SA) magazine asking fort this information: Why human body development and maturation take much longer time than their counterparts in the non-human species? SA sent me a reply one year later. Yet, SA did not offer an explanation. SA editors advised me simply to look up Anthropology Websites for possible answer. The Scientific American magazine mentioned reply to my question was not helpful.

THE NEED FOR A COMPLEX THINKING APPROACH

Even if these two sciences have a solid bio-genetic explanation for that, this should not discourage scientists and researchers outside of the sciences of the genetics and biology to look for other potential or even crucial determinant factors which could also *be involved* in the making of the longer human lifespan in question. This is quite legitimate in a time when scientists and researchers are more and more convinced of the complex nature of the factors which may co-influence particularly a given human phenomenon. The French sociologist and philosopher, Edgar Morin, speaks of the necessity of the adoption today by modern scientists, researchers and scholars of what he calls *the complex thinking approach* (Morin 1990). In other words, scholars, scientists and researchers should avoid the use of strict simplist reductionist approach in their study particularly of human phenomena which are complex by their own nature. My HS thesis in this book is in line with Morin's perspective. On the one hand, to explain the distinct human longer lifespan solely by bio-genetic factors is a very reductionist approach. It can hardly see, beyond its frontiers, any plausible influential other factor(s) which should seriously be taken into consideration in the understanding and the explanation of the human longer lifespan. On the other hand, my search for the causes behind the phenomenon of the human longer lifespan has shown, as outlined in previous chapters, that there are more factors involved in human longer lifespan than the mere narrow territory of the bio-genetics of humans. As pointed out earlier, I use the HS perspective in order to help understand and explain the cause(s) behind the longer lifespan which the members of the human race are privileged to have[3].

As argued before, HS need longer human lifespan to fully grow, develop and mature. Based on that great importance of the role HS to the unique destiny of humankind, I could restate the former correlation: on the one side, humans are absolutely unique because of their enormous skills in the use of HS. On the other side, they are also considerably unique in their relative longer lifespan. Is there a link between these two unique human characteristics? And what kind of a relationship is there between them? Let us take a look, through some illustrative examples, how the presence of HS in humans would necessarily require longer lifespan for them. In modern social science terminology, there appears to be a strong correlation between these two human characteristics. I have briefly explained that strong correlation in the first chapter of this book. In order to consolidate the scientific credibility of the correlation, there is a need for more elaboration on this matter.

THE PACE OF GROWTH AND MATURITY OF HS

As emphasized throughout this book, the human species is distinguishable by its possession and use of the complex system of HS. As mentioned before, the HS need longer time to grow, evolve and reach their maximum maturation .For instance, while the growth and maturity of the human body reach their peak around the age 25, the beginning of the development of mature complex thinking (part of the HS) hardly appears before the human individual reaches his/her 20 years. But an adequate real mature human thought does not often materialize before the person reaches his/her forties. And the peak maturity of human thought usually crystallizes by the age of forty and beyond (Gardner 1982: 357, Hunt 1982: 279). All this shows that the growth, the evolution and the reaching of final maturity in human thought require indeed longer lifespan for humans. In other words, the development and the full maturity of the world of the HS *need roughly more than twice* of the years required for the growth and the complete maturation of the human body.

This state of HS slow growth and maturation appears to be the outcome of an initial slow innate nature of the human brain growth and development parts relevant for the full use of the complex world of the human HS. It has to do here with a sort of an innate bio-genetico-neuro make up design of the human brain that needs longer time to use and develop fully the entire spectrum of human activities associated with and elaborated by the human HS. This sort of innate slow tendency for human thought growth, development and maturation is compatible with the impact of the dual human identity (body and HS) on the slow pace of the human body growth, development and maturation as shown before. In other words, the bipolar human identity (body and HS) does not only predispose the human body for a slow pace of growth, development and maturation, but it does as well affect the slow pace of human thought growth, development and maturation. As such, I can say that the dual human identity has *a global impact* on the slow pace of growth development and maturation of both the body and the HS.

YEARS DIFFERENCE BETWEEN THE CHILD'S MUSCULAR AND LINGUISTIC DEVELOPMENT

In order to be more specific on the gap in years between these two realms of human development, I compare here the child's body pace of growth with that of his/her linguistic development in order to underline the slower development of the human HS. At the age of five months the child can roll over his/her body at all sides. When he/she reaches eight months he/she can sit alone and at eleven months he/she can sit alone and at eleven months he/she can stand by himself/herself and at his/her first birthday the child is able to walk alone(Encyclopedia of Psychology 1973: 43).

As to the development of the child's language, it goes through several phases. Observations show that the child begins the process of vocalization and cooing between four and eight weeks of age whether he/she is alone or with others. Between 12 and 16 months the child's first words appear as imitations of adult speaking, usually nouns with emotional significance "Mama", "Daddy". At the age of two years the child has a good understanding of language and he/she can in general make two and three words phrases. Between four and five years of age the child uses more adultlike grammar with some complex constructions still missing. His/her vocabulary at this age is between 5000 and 7000 words. He/she masters the grammar language around the age of 12 years (Ibid).

These two examples show that the development and maturity of the child's language - the most important of all HS- need much longer time than the growth and the maturity of his/her body which permits him/her to stand and walk alone at a very early age. The human being's possession of HS and their implications on the behaviour of the human species lead inevitably to the discussion of the brain/the mind, because the latter is the mileu per excellence for the development and maturity of the human HS.

THE BRAIN/MIND AND THE HUMAN LONGER LIFESPAN

In order to explain this discrepancy in the pace of growth and maturation between these two realms of the human entity, I can refer to what may be called an objective descriptive approach which is widely used by modern science in order to understand and explain phenomena. Scientists are of the view that the members of the human species need longer lifespan because of their brain/mind. The explanation of this relationship has been described as follows:

1. As underlined in the first chapter of this book in particular, observations show that the growth and maturation of the organs of the human body take a much longer time (in years) than the growth and maturation of the organs of the bodies of the other living species. Scientists have explained this difference by the presence of the brain /mind in the human species. Because of this slow pace of growth and maturation of the organs of the human body, the individual members of the human species will, therefore, require longer lifespan, so the organs of their bodies can reach their peak of growth and maturation. What is at stake here is the human biology itself. Its processes of growth and maturation are greatly put off in comparison with those of the non-human biology. There is a fundamental question which has to be raised here. It is a Basic Research question: what does the human brain/mind (HS) have to do to be able to slow down the biological processes on the human body? Unfortunately, most biologists have confined themselves to the simple description of the working of the human biology. Consequently, the other factors - which may be involved in these matters and they are beyond the frontiers of human biology - have hardly been raised.

2. Man's brain/mind has made what sociologists call socialization (basically, through HS) a very long process in terms of the number of years needed for its accomplishment when compared with the length of the process of socialization among the rest of the other living species. The human socialization consists of the individual's learning the HS of his/her milieu/society such as language, religious beliefs, customs, cultural values and norms and the heritage of knowledge/science. With successful socialization, the individual becomes a full member in his/her milieu/society. In other words, the complete and successful socialization makes the individual assimilate entirely into the melting pot of their own society. This can hardly be achieved within a very short time. But rather, it could last until the age of adolescence. The lengthy period of human socialization is due largely to the slow pace, the difficulty and the complexity of mastering and assimilating the HS of society into the basic personality of the individuals. Human socialization is a continuing process and it has practically no end particularly in ever changing modern societies. But again, there is need to go beyond the simple sociological description of the process of socialization .We need to ask: what is in the HS

that makes them not easy to be learned and mastered quicker and at an earlier age?. In other words, what special about them that makes them slower than the biological processes in their growth and maturation? Is there any hidden dimension in them that both modern natural and social sciences have not dealt with? I already mentioned the HS innate tendency to be slower in their growth, development and maturation. This could be explained by the parameters of the dual human identity (body and HS). It could be argued that for human survival purposes, priority is given first to body growth, development and maturation. This explains the big slower pace of HS growth, development and maturation. The given priority to the human body growth, development and maturation should also help explain, for instance, the late coming of mature human thinking which usually takes place after the human body has reached its peak of growth, development and maturation around the age of 25 years (Rischer, Easton 1992: 603). In other words, once the business of the human body's growth, development and maturation is fully achieved, the gate becomes strongly wide open for the great development, growth and maturation of HS in their various and complex manifestations in human cultures.

CULTURAL DETERMINISM AND THE HUMAN LIFESPAN

On the one hand, as it has just been shown, the longer lifespan of members of the human species is to be accounted for, in great part, by the factor of the HS underlined in the entire book. There is some sort of *cultural determinism* behind the average longer lifespan of the members of the human species. On the other hand, living species which don't have HS don't need as a matter of fact longer lifespan; because their biological and physical growth are terminated in shorter periods. So that each species could fulfill its functions at the appropriate age and subsequently it guarantees the continuity of its offspring in spite of its very short lifespan. But the distinction of the human species by the HS has made the human species' longer lifespan necessary for its own survival. This has been achieved by two ways:

(a) As pointed out earlier, the presence of the brain/ mind in the human species delays by many years the achievement of full growth and development of the human organic body. While the maturity of the body and organs of certain animals can be attained at the age of one or two years, the maturity of the body and organs of humans can hardly be fully realized before the age of fifteen years. This bio- physiological fact requires that humans must live longer in order to fulfill their full bio-physiological growth and maturity and be able to secure the continuing existence of the human species through the reproductive process.

(b) As underlined before, the nature of growth and maturation of HS is much slower than that of the growth and maturation of the human body. In order for the HS to perform their full and complex functions and roles in the individual's life and in the development of human societies and civilizations it becomes compelling that the members of the human species have longer lifespan. The time factor in years and decades is so crucial for HS full development of the human HS. In other words, the full blown maturity of the human HS is not only space (social milieu) dependent, but it is also strongly *time dependent*. It becomes, therefore, a compelling necessity for humans to enjoy longer lifespan. In modern social science terms, there is a strong correlation between the presence of the human HS and the need for longer lifespan.

It is evident from the analysis just presented, that the longer human life-span is largely a response to the needs of HS. That is, it could be said that those needs of the HS have dictated, so to speak, a special bio-chemico-genetico-neurological structure of the human species design in order to per-mit the members of the human species to enjoy longer lifespan than the other living species which are deprived of HS. As mentioned before in previous chapters, my perspective is somewhat *opposite to that of Sociobiology* which claims that numerous human social behaviours are triggered by the genes and the biology of the human body.

My analysis here shows rather that it is *the cultural factors* which have in turn influenced the very action of the biology and genes of the human spe-cies. It has to do here of what I may call *Culturalbiology*. That makes the HS concept visibly transdisciplinary which is good to deal with matters between disciplines trough out different disciplines and beyond each discipline. The final goal of this concept is to understand the present world by the establish-ment of the human knowledge unity (Nicolescu 1996: 66). Thus, the HS concept could be used to explain the socio-cultural as well as the biological dimensions of the human entity. The thesis developed in this chapter is quite compatible with the new emerging scientific outlook which calls upon scien-tists, scholars and researchers to expand their visions beyond the narrow views through which they look at and explain complex phenomena. They need rather to adopt *transdisciplinary views*. The latter study phenomena as complex entities which are, at one level, influenced by different factors and, on another level, the influential factors are influencing and influenced agents at the same time (Morin 1990).

BIOLOGY, GENETICS AND HS

The strong correlation established so far between the longer human lifespan and the HS is hardly mentioned in the enormous corpus of modern science in general. As pointed out before, both genetics and biology make no reference to the role of HS in the length of the human lifespan. For these two branches of the so-called exact sciences, the question of the longer human lifespan has to be analysed and explained only in genetical and biological terms. This does not mean, however, that biologists and geneticists don't make any mention of HS. On the contrary, they even speak of HS as what makes the human race human (Rischer, Easton 1992: 603). But, nonetheless, they neither look at human biology and genetics through those humanizing HS as shown in my concept of Cultural biology, nor do they say very much about the relationship between HS and human biology and genetics let alone the very nature of HS as well as why they grow and mature slowly. In other words, *there is hardly any real help* one could seek from these two branches of modern science in order to answer some of the Basic Research questions on the essential nature of HS.

MODERN SOCIAL SCIENCES AND THE MISSING TRANSCENDENTALITY

When I examine the profile of modern Western social sciences I hardly find reference to the concept of the transcendentality of HS as used in this book. As explained previously, HS transcendentality is displayed in the following features: (1) HS have neither volume nor weight (2) HS have potential long / eternal lifespan. (3) HS have potential rapid/instant mobility through space and time. (4) HS charge humans with fantastic motivation and energy that make them so powerful and defying like *metaphysical forces.*

As part of the notion of culture, as defined by the British anthropologist Edward B. Tylor, HS have received a special attention particularly from the disciplines of anthropology and sociology. Both have extensively studied religion, language, cultural values and norms, magic, science, thought, myths, as seen particularity in other chapters. Countless anthropological and sociological studies have been written about the functions, the pace of change, the diffusion etc. of those HS in human societies. Contemporary anthropologists and sociologists have widely used the concept of culture/HS in order to analyze and explain individual and collective social behaviours in human societies. For instance, common cultural values and religious beliefs in societies are used to account for the patterned collective social behaviours of individuals of different systems of personalities. HS are, thus, fundamental basis for the social solidarity and, subsequently, for the emergence of the phenomena of human societies themselves. As such, the concept of HS is crucially important in the study of the dynamics of human behaviours be that of the individual or of the collectivity. In contrast to non-human behaviour which are basically determined by the biological instincts, most human individual and collective social behaviours are strongly oriented and shaped by cultural factors. All this shows, beyond any doubt, that *HS are serious regulating agents of human behaviours* in both the individual and the collective sense.

This type of analysis of the impact of HS on human behaviours is the common approach adopted by modern social sciences. It may be called a cultural behaviourist approach. The latter looks at HS as external stimuli out there in the social milieu with little interest paid, if any, to the internal side of those stimuli. Behavioural psychologists are well known for their disdain of studying the unobservable factors which could affect human behaviour[4].

Their uneasiness with the disciplines of cognitive psychology (the study of the internal state of the human mind) and psychoanalysis (the study of the impact of unconsciousness on human behaviour)appears to be associated with the study of the potential hidden dimensions of HS like the transcendental features referred to in this chapter and the previous ones. For example, a review of the countless Introductory text books of sociology in the USA confirms the absence of reference to the transcendental dimensions of HS. Most of these introductory textbooks have a chapter about culture where definitions of cultural concepts are given, explained, discussed and sometimes applied. But in spite of this, I don't recall yet having seen any of those many introductory textbooks which has made reference to the transcendental dimensions of HS, as outlined in this book (White 1973).

This state of affaires could be accounted for by the general *spirit of Western modern science*. On the one hand, this science is more inclined to study the observable, the measurable and the quantifiable phenomena. As such, it has a sort of a hostile attitude toward those phenomena which don't qualify to be studied by the rather Positivist approach. On the other hand, devising an appropriate new methodology becomes a big obstacle for those few conventional modern social scientists who recognize the legitimacy of those commonly non-observable, non-measurable and non-quantifiable phenomena. In contrast to this, my transdisciplinary HS concept is potentially qualified to give importance to both objective and subjective dimensions of HS as strong human parameters/determinants of individual behaviours as well as the dynamics of human societies and civilizations.

SOCIAL SCIENCES UNFIT FOR HS STUDY

As shown in this chapter and in others in this book, the total failure of bio-genetical sciences to deal with HS as such and the partial failure of modern social sciences to address the transcendental /spiritual/ metaphysical dimensions of HS make both of them *hardly fit* to come to our help for the understanding of the HS from within.

From a methodological viewpoint, there is pressing need for the discovery of this *'hidden dimension' of the HS*. I have established in the preceding pages here and in previous chapters that there is a strong correlation between human HS and the human longer lifespan. In modern social sciences, correlational relationships between phenomena are usually interpreted in two ways: (1) direct cause effect relationship. This means one phenomenon is the direct cause of the other phenomenon. (2) non-direct cause-effect relationship. This implies that the phenomenon in question is not directly caused by the other phenomenon in correlation, but rather by the so-called intervening variable. The latter is a factor/cause different from the phenomenon in correlation.

It could be said that both modern bio-genetical sciences and social sciences have, in general, remained *silent* on the direct or non-direct cause (s) which make (s) the growth and the full maturity of HS take much longer time in terms of the number of years than the growth and the full maturity of the organs of the human body. Social scientists are certainly aware of this factor. But one hardly can find in the vast social science literature the cause-effect or the intervening variable explanation(s) of this time difference in growth and maturity between the two realms of the human entity: the bio-physical human body and the HS. What one finds, instead, in this enormous social sciences literature is a "descriptive approach" statements and analyses. In other words, HS are described as they could be observed and analyzed objectively and externally without making reference neither to why they grow slower or last longer (human ideas, thought) than the human bio-physical organs... nor do they consider the plausibility that HS may have 'hidden dimension' which is beyond the objective observable field of the Positivist science[5] . The latter is well known for its full denial of transcendental/ metaphysical features of HS whose importance is stressed throughout the chapters of this book.

THE ISLAMIC PERSPECTIVE AS AN ALTERNATIVE

There is, therefore, a genuine need for the adoption of an approach different from the prevailing conventional one in modern social sciences. It should be a balanced approach: it studies HS from within and from without. It focuses equally on the external (the observable, the objective...) as well as the internal (subjective, transcendental, metaphysical) dimensions of HS In short, we need a perspective which could help us answer some of the questions about HS which modern social sciences either have not raised or have not been interested to answer them. I have chosen the Islamic perspective for this task. There are three reasons for that. First, my transdisciplinary HS concept includes religious vision and perception in its perspective. Second. I have been working on HS for over eighteen years. My Islamic perspective is quite present in my published work (Dhaouadi 1996) and in the last two chapters.. Second, the Qur'an, Islam's Holy Book, is full of verses which speak of dualism as a common feature of all the universe' phenomena. From this point of view, the nature of HS should not only be of one sided nature: external, objective and observable. This view misses the inside hidden (subjective, the transcendental...) dimension of the nature of HS. According to the Quran, the internal nature of HS is heavily invested with the divine spark as it has been explained in part II of this work. Thus, modern social sciences' focus on the study of HS from the outside is hardly objective scientifically. The credibility of the entire corpus of modern social sciences' concepts, theories, paradigms etc. about HS is expected, therefore, to be very much lacking. The inclusion of *Islamic insights* in the elaboration of my HS concept is part of making it transdisciplinary.

In using the Islamic perspective in the analysis of HS I have two goals in mind which are fully compatible with the thesis of this chapter and the entire book: (1) the acquisition of more knowledge about the inside nature of HS. As seen, they develop and mature much slower than the bio-physical human organs. Then, the legitimate question which should be raised is: what is in the nature of HS that makes them slower in their development and maturation? (2) could the findings from question (1) explain or make sense out (Verstehen) of the strong correlation between the HS on the one hand, and the longer lifespan enjoyed by the members of the human species, on the other? The performance of the Islamic perspective in the exploration of HS in this chapter and others of this book is to be measured and tested by the quality of answers it offers to these two major questions.

HUMAN NATURE IN THE QUR'AN

In order to identify the nature of HS from an Islamic perspective, I found no better reference than the Qur'an itself which is Islam's first authoritative reference text. There are many verses in the Muslim Holy Book that speak with clarity of human nature. I have chosen only two verses which do describe in full the basic components of human nature. The two verses in question are: Behold ! thy Lord said to the angels : 1 am about to create man, from sounding clay from mud moulded into shape. When 1 have fashioned him (in due proportion) and breathed into him of My spirit, fall ye down in obeisance unto him) (19). *Human nature*, according to these two verses, *is dualistic* in nature. It is made up of clay and the divine breathed spirit.

As to which one of these two components is *more important* in the making of human nature, one interpretation of these two verses may allow one to assert that the Our'an gives more importance to the side of *the divine breathed spirit into the human entity*. Since the angels were asked by God to prostrate to Adam immediately after, and not before, the divine spirit was breathed into him. The angels' prostrating act before Adam is seen as a symbolic sign of respect to this godly new privileged creature who has been the only creature to receive a special divine breathed spirit. This Qur'anic position in favour of the spiritual dimension of human nature is a fundamental permanent principle which runs throughout the entire text of the Qur'an. We are told again and again in the verses of the 114 Surahs/chapters of the Qur'an, that human individuals, groups, collectivities, societies and civilizations *can achieve excellence* only when their *divine breathed spirit* overdominates the materialistic (clay) side of their human nature.

THE IMAGE OF MAN IN THE QUR'AN

So far I have established two major observations:

1. There is a strong correlation between HS and longer human lifespan.
2. From Qur'anic viewpoint, HS are of divine origin. Consequently, they show transcendental manifestations in human action.

The question now is this: is it possible to rely on these two observations in order to account for the longer human lifespan? The Islamic perspective has its own view of the creation of man as well as his image in the world of countless living species. First, the Qur'an offers its version of Adam's creation. This is spelled out in full in many verses of the Qur'an. The event of the human creation was the outcome of the interaction between the physical (the clay) and the metaphysical (the breathed divine spirit). In other words, human creation was the result of a contact between matter and the divine spirit.

Second, The Qur'anic text addresses the consequences of the event of the human creation. That is, what did happen when the fusion between matter and the divine spark took place? As an answer to such a question; the Qur 'an speaks highly of the new creature (Adam); because the matter (the clay) is no longer just a matter. *It has now part of the divine spirit.* In modern terms, the new creature is no longer a pure quantitative (matter/clay) being. With the breathed divine spirit into him he is now a qualitative creature as well.

Third, the Qur'anic text does not only point out explicitly to these two poles of the human entity but *it sides strongly*, at the same time, more *with man's qualitative dimension* whose origin is the divine spirit. As mentioned before, the divine order to the angels to prostrate to Adam came after, and not before, the divine spirit was breathed into the new creature: "When 1 have fashioned him (in due proportion) and breathed into him of My spirit, fall ye down in obeisance unto him". In Qur'anic terms, the most important dimension of the dualistic human entity is that one which had directly resulted from the breathed divine spirit. This is in full logic with the Qur'anic epistemology. In the Qur'an, God is the ultimate of the ultimates in wisdom, knowledge, creation, action, mercy, perfection. So, a little spark of His spirit breathed into Adam in-clay shape is bound to radically transform the quality of that dead shaped clay. This great transformation has not only made man the master over the rest of the other creatures but also God's representative (khalifa) on this planet. He is superior over other species not because of his quantitative dimension (physical size, height etc...) but basically because of *his qualitative dimension*: the special set of HS .This is the overwhelming position of today social and human sciences (Dortier 2004: 398).

DUALISTIC HUMAN ENTITY AND LONGER LIFESPAN

How does this Qur'anic dualistic image of man help explain the longer human lifespan? It has been emphasized throughout this chapter and others that humans live longer because their HS develop and mature slower than the bio-physical organs of the human body. As such, the humans need to live longer in order that their HS could achieve their full development and maturity. How can we use the Qur'anic dualistic view of man to account for the human longer lifespan?

In order to answer this fundamental question I confine myself to the use of my concept of HS as elaborated in this chapter and the entire book. On the other hand, I use a Qur'anico-metaphysico-philosophical vision to help understand and explain how HS could play a decisive role in the making of the longer human lifespan. This approach is *anti-Positivist* in nature. There should be no surprise in the adoption of such a vision. It is argued throughout this work that HS are heavily impregnated with transcendentality. The latter can hardly be accepted let alone be studied, by empirical Positivist science. I would like to discuss the relationship between HS and the human longer lifespan away form the narrow logic of strict Empiricism and Positivism. *HS have transcendental features*. The transcendental universe is different from the five senses human experience world. The transcendental universe has its own logic, rules and dynamics. My Qur'anico-methaphisico-philosophical approach is greatly free from the constraints of empiricism and Positivism. The latter are ill-equiped for the study of the transcendentality of HS. The discussion of HS here is beyond the reach of Positivist science.

Using my transdisciplinary approach, I confine myself here to the discussion of *four ideas/ hypotheses* about the links between HS and longer human lifespan.

1. It could be argued that HS grow and mature slower because their nature is more complex than the nature of the bio-physical organs of the human body. In the words of Cassirer "Man is compensated by *another gift* which he

alone develops and which bears no analogy to anything in organic nature. Not immediately but by a very complex and difficult process of thought, he arrives at the idea of abstract space" (Cassirer 1970: 48).. So humans need to live longer because the complexity of their HS requires more time for the realization of full development and maturity of the complex HS. While the complexity assumption is acceptable as a tangible and objective tool of analysis of the correlation between HS and the longer human lifespan, it does not, however, put an end to many of the questions which could still be raised in this regard. For instance, what do we mean by the complexity of HS? What makes them more complex than the bio-physical organs of the human body? Are they more complex because of their metaphysical/divine origin? The answers to these questions are hardly to be sought within the framework of empirico-positivist science. What is needed here is a perspective that sheds light and improves our understanding of phenomena which Empiricism and Positivism can practically offer no help. *Insights from religion, philosophy and metaphysics* should be, therefore, welcomed as long as they bring us closer to the understanding of the nature of HS and their special impact on the behaviour and destiny of the human species.

2. The correlation between HS and the longer human lifespan could be examined within a parapsycholoqical framework. That is, how spirit affects matter. The Qur'anic version of Adam's creation is a classical example of the interaction between matter and spirit. Adam is the outcome of the combination of the clay and the divine spirit. As pointed out, the breathed divine spirit had transformed the quality of the New human being. The divine spark had endowed him with transcendental characteristics. I have shown how HS are heavily impregnated with transcendentality. It could also be argued here that HS don't have only longer/eternal lifespan in themselves, but they also transfer this quality to matter. That is, the human body's lifespan is extended. There appears to be unavoidable mutual influence between spirit and matter once they are fused together in one entity like Adam's. So the side affect of the HS longer/eternal lifespan is carried in a limited manner, so to speak, to the bio-physical side (clay, matter) of the human entity. The parapsychological view of longer human lifespan could hardly be in disagreement with the religio-philosophico-metaphysical insights about the role of HS on the human destiny (Pedler 1981).

3. As seen before, HS are the greater important part of the breathed divine spirit into man. They are part of what I have called *the qualitative dimension* of the dualistic humane entity. From a Qur'anic point of view, the divine spirit, including especially *HS is the best side of man's duality*. Without the divine spirit, man could not have been God's only representative on earth. But this has its own consequences. As it has been emphasized, the full development and maturity of HS require longer time. In other words, humans have to pay a price for the gift of the enormous use of HS.

The price here is time in years and decades which the full development of both of their human body and their HS would necessarily need. But this price has its positive aspect. It has allowed humans to have longer lifespan. There is no doubt that human HS are at the core of man's qualitative dimension. Therefore, there is a strong need for more time in years and decades to pay for that qualitative side. So the full development and maturity of the entire human entity would be materialized. As such, the longer human lifespan ought not be only examined through bio- genetic determinism but it deserves to be analyzed as well by the culturo-religio-philosophico-metaphysical insights.

4. From a Qur'anic point of view, the origin of the longer human life is the breathed divine spirit into humans. There are two manifestations to this. On the one hand, as shown in the preceding pages, there is strong correlation between longer human lifespan and the presence of HS among the members of the human species. HS take much longer time (in years and decades) to see themselves reach their peak in growth, development and maturity. This has made humans enjoy longer lifespan as compared with shorter lifespans of the members of the many other living species. That is, the impact here of HS on the lengthening of the human lifespan is a limited one.

On the other hand, the Qur'anic text is quite explicit that the breathed divine spirit had endowed *man* to become ultimately an *eternal being*. Of course, he is not bio-physically eternal in this world. He just lives longer life than the other species. But he is eternal after Resurrection. According to the Qur'an, he will live forever in Paradise or in Hell. There is no mention in the Qur'anic text either of the Resurrection of non-human species or of their eternal life afterwards. This difference between humans and non- humans in the length of lifespan in this world and in the eternal life after Resurrection appears to be strongly related to the special divine spirit which only humans have received, according to the Qur'an. This divine spirit has made man both God's khalifa in this world and accountable for his action in front of God who will examine the humans' accountability on the Day of Judgement after which humans will live for ever in Paradise or in Hell. As argued throughout this chapter, HS are outstanding components of the breathed divine spirit. They are decisive forces for the longer lifespan of humans and because of them, humans are also held responsible for their action in this life for which they receive either eternal life in Paradise or in Hell. In other words, HS can be seen first as the main forces behind the relative longer human lifespan and, second, as, the principal factors, from a Qur'anic viewpoint, that make humans legitimate for eternal life after Resurrection. Thus, the correlation between HS and the span of human existence appears to be *strong* both in the relative and the absolute sense of the length of lifespan.

REFERENCES

Ali, A.Y. (1989). *The Meaning of The Holy Qur'an*. Brentwood, Maryland: Amana Corporation, Surah XV, 28-29, p.625.

Al-Qurtubi, Abou Abdullah. (1967). *Al Jamia Li-Ahkam al Qur'an* (in Arabic). Cairo: Dar al Kitab al Arabi li Ahiba'a wa al Nnashri, *X*, 24-25.

Al-Razi, F. (1981). *Tafsir Al Qur'an* (in Arabic). Beirut: Dar Al Fikr, *X*, 185-186.

Annajar, Z. (2002). *The Quran's Scientific Inimitability* (in Arabic), Part I. (3rd ed.). Cairo: Shorouk International Library.

Assad, M. (1980). *The Message of the Qur'an*. Gibraltar: Dar Al-Andalus.

Baert, P. (1998). *Social Theory in the Twentieth Century*. New York: New York University Press.

Balibar, E. (1979). *Cinq Etudes du Matérialisme Historique*. Paris: Maspéro.

Ben Achour, M.T. (no date). *Tafsir Al Tahrir wa al Tanwir* (in Arabic). Tunis: Dar al Tunisiyah li-Annashr, *XIII*.

Bly, B.M., and Rumechatt, D. (Eds.). (1999). *Cognitive Science*. San Diago: Academic Press.

Bonnell, V., and Hunt, L. (Eds) (1999). *Beyond the Cultural Turn*. Berkeley: University of California Press.

Cassirer, E. (1970). *An Essay On Man*. New York: Bantam Books.

Crane, D. (Ed.). (1995). *The Sociology of Culture*. Oxford (UK): Blackwell.

Dhaouadi, M. (1996). *Toward Islamic Sociology of Cultural Symbols*. Kuala Lumpur: A.S. Noordeen.

Dortier, J-F. (2004). *L'homme cet étrange animal*. Auxerre, Cedex: Sciences Humaines Editions.

Encyclopedia of Psychology. (1973). Guilford, CN: The Dushkin Publihing Group, Inc.

Gardner, H. (1982). *Art, Mind and Brains: A Cognitive Approach to Creativity*. New York: Basic Books, Inc, and (1982). Hunt, M. *The Universe Within: A New Science Explores the Human Mind*. New York: Simons and Schuster.

Morin, E. (1990). *Introduction à la pensée complexe*. Paris: E.S.F.

Pedler, K. (1981). *Mind Over Matter: A Scientific Yiew of The Paranormal*. London: Thames Methuen.

Philips, D.C. (1985). *Philosophy, Science and Social Inquiry*. New York: Pergamon Press.

Qutub, S. (1985). *Zilal al Qur'an* (in Arabic). Beirut: Dar al Shark, *XII, X, IIVB*.

Smelser, N., Smelser, W. *Personality and Social Systems*. New York: John Wiley and Sons.

Rischer, C.E., and Easton, Th.A. (1992). *Focus on Human Biology*. New York: Harper Collins Publishers Inc.

Spillman, L. (Ed.). (2007). *Cultural Sociology*. Oxford (UK): Blacwell Publishing.

The World Almanac and Book of Facts. (1994).

Time Magazine. (1995, March 6). p.45 and *Al Wassat Magazine* (in Arabic). (1995 March 6). p.68.

Wilson, E. (1975). *Sociobiology: The New Synthesis*. Cambridge, MA: Harvard University Press.

White, L. (1973). *The Concept of Culture*. Edina: Alpha Editions.

NOTES

1. This strong correlation between HS and longer human lifespan is found in the following study: Attendance at Cultural Events, Reading books or Periodicals, and Making Music or Singing in a Choir as Derterminants for Survival: Swedish Interview Survey of Living Conditions, British Medical Journal,Vol.313,21-28. December1996, pp.1577.Conclusion: attendance at cultural events may have a positive influence on survival and mortality.

2. Contemporary anthropology and sociology are the two disciplines which have studied culture more than any other discipline in the social and human sciences. But, both have failed to ask and especially to answer those kind of questions about the very deep internal nature of

culture. Some of the few anthropologists and sociologists who came litlle close to those questions and answers ended up using vague and confusing terms that have kept anthropology and sociology at a distance from dealing with the substantive and profound nature of culture. For those few, culture is seen as superorganic, suprabiological, an abstraction, as having no ontological reality or belonging to extrasomatic context (White 1973:10,24,29,47).

3. The French monthly magazine *Sciences Humaines* has made a recent brief review (No.139, June 2003, pp .16-24) of research on human nature from the point of view of Evolutionary Psychology (EP).It is shown that EP has two versions of human nature:
a)-The hard version sees human instincts as programs of rigid and very specific unvariable rigid behaviours, (p.23).
b)-The soft or moderate version believes that human nature does exist, but it expresses it self in terms of propensities, potentialities, inclinations and tendencies rather than in terms of rigid programs (p.23). Obviously, this version gives a large role to culture in the determination of human behaviours. As such, it does not come close to our concept of the centrality of CS (culture) in the making of human nature itself. That special strong centrality of CS does not only greatly determine human behaviours but also the bio-physical destiny (longer lifespan) of humans as argued in this chapter and the book in general.

4. The German pholosopher Nietsches (1844-1900) is classical example.

5. The French Social determinist sociologist Emile Durkheim and the Behaviourist American psychologist B.F. Skinner are leading figures in modern behavioural social sciences in their opposition to non-objectivized factors as determinants of human behaviours.

Chapter Eight

Social Science Illiteracy of the Other Underdevelopment in Post-Colonial Societies

THE WIDE ILLITERACY ON THE OTHER UNDERDEVELOPMENT

In dealing with the phenomenon of underdevelopment in the Third World, during the first and the second modernity's eras, Western social scientists have tended to *confine themselves* to the socio-economico-political sides of the phenomenon of underdevelopment (Jacquemot 1981, Bauman 2005).The accumulated quantity of Western social sciences literature on underdevelopment since the Second World War is impressive indeed. *Yet, there is hardly any reference to the other sides of underdevelopment (The Other Underdevelopment/OU)* (Piterse 2001). That is, the psycho-cultural underdevelopment, according to my own conceptualization of this subcategory of the larger phenomenon of the Third World underdevelopment. As mentioned in chapter II in Part I, we measure the OU in developing societies by such behavioral/psychological manifestations like the desire to imitate the West, suffering from inferiority complex as well as by using Western linguistico-cultural borrowing like languages English, French...) instead of native ones. Third World heavy dependency on Western modern science and knowledge, the wide diffusion of Western cultural values in developing countries...etc... As such, The OU is seen in my perspective as having largely resulted from Western imperial domination of Asian, African and Latin American societies in contemporary times.[1] That is, *the OU is an underdevelopment which strongly touches the universe of the national HS of developing countries.*

In response to this academic and intellectual illiteracy silence vis-à-vis the OU, I have set out here and elsewhere to explore this *"Forgotten Under-*

development" (Dhaouadi 2002) in a rather operational systematic framework. As expected, one can hardly seek any direct help from Western or Third World Western-oriented social sciences in going about defining, conceptualizing and theorizing in this field of research. The illiteracy of both of these social sciences on the OU constitutes in itself a strange phenomenon which needs an explanation. I shall attempt to do that in the last part of this chapter.

THE BIPOLAR NATURE OF THE OU

As a phenomenon, The OU is viewed as having two major components (1) The culturo-linguistic underdevelopment component and (2) The psychological underdevelopment component. The OU is, thus, *a psycho-culturo-linguistic underdevelopment* in nature as it will be argued throughout this chapter. In order to do that I discuss, on the one hand, the nature of each one of the two components and, on the other, attempt to look at them as two interdependent components which interact ultimately with each other in a reciprocal pattern. Therefore, OU can be looked at and conceptualized as a psycho-culturo-linguistic-system.

THE CULTURAL LINGUISTIC UNDERDEVELOPMENT

Culture, as defined by Edward B. Tylor 1871, is seen especially by modern anthropologists and sociologists as a vital force of human society existence. Society's dynamics depends greatly on the state of its cultural forces. As seen before, Tylor's concept of culture does not include language, though without the latter we can hardly conceive of culture in its human broad sense. As such, *language is the cornerstone* for the emergence of the phenomenon of the complex human culture or HS which are seen as the most distinctive features of the human species. So, they are so basic to the human identity. Understanding Third World underdevelopment remains incomplete and shortsighted without paying adequate attention to its HS aspects of underdevelopment. Third World HS underdevelopment is but one dimension of its global (socio-economic, political dimensions, etc...) underdevelopment and it can be measured by three manifestations:

1) Linguistic underdevelopment

I define linguistic underdevelopment as, on the one hand, the widespread use of a foreign language/languages in a given society and, on the other hand, the under usage (the less than full use) of society's own native language(s) (spoken/written or both). The danger of linguistic underdevelopment has to be taken very seriously, because it has a strong negative impact on languages' cultures as well as on the very continuing existence of underdeveloping languages (Wurn 2001). In today's Third World, linguistic underdevelopment can best be illustrated by the African continent case.

a) Black Africa's linguistic underdevelopment:

As a result of Western imperialism in Africa since The 15th century, English, French, Portuguese and Spanish have become the official languages of most countries of today's Black Africa. There are nearly as many independent African states which use English as there are states that use French as their official languages. The total number of those countries amounts to 38 which constitute the majority of the African states of the Black continent (Frgs 1984: 164-183). It is because of this linguistic fact that Africa is so often divided today into *two Africas*: 1) English speaking Africa and 2) French speaking Africa. To name just a few of these countries I can mention Uganda, Ghana, Nigeria, Liberia and Sierra Leona which belong to English speaking Africa while Senegal, Tchad, Guinea, Congo and Zaire are representative of French speaking Africa. Portugal's earlier colonization in the continent has led to the spread use of Portuguese in such countries like Mozambique, Angola and Guinea-Bissau where Portuguese is still the official language of these independent states. Compared to the wide use of English and French in Black Africa, the Portuguese use is considerably limited. It is adopted only in five countries as an official language. Finally Spanish, as an official language, is found only in Equatorial Guinea. As such the overspread use of these languages particularly in various modern sectors of these societies constitutes *a linguistic underdevelopment*. In other words, native languages are not given the opportunity to be fully used in all walks of life. Their growth and their maturity are, therefore, bound to be hampered and underdeveloped. *The general acute linguistic underdevelopment in Black Africa* should not, however, be explained only by Western imperialism but also by in-built internal difficult linguistic situations which characterize most of these countries. On the one side, there is hardly any common language/ dialect in each of those societies which is understood and acceptable to all clans, tribes and groups. On the other hand, the language(s)/dialect(s) is often limited to the oral form. As such, its full use falls short of meeting the modern aspirations of the new African states like self-management of modern structures and institutions in their own societies. This delicate linguistic state in today's Black Africa should be meaningful in any rigorous attempt to understand the special nature of the complex problems of underdevelopment facing those nations. That is to say, the challenges they face in the battle against underdevelopment are not limited only to the socio-economic dimensions. *Their underdevelopment is global in nature* (Dhaouadi 2002). Their psycho-culturo-symbolic underdevelopment is a fundamental component of their broad underdevelopment as this chapter attempts to make clear.

b) North Africa's linguistic underdevelopment:

Furthermore, the North African societies (Algeria, Tunisia and Morocco) can hardly be exempted as well from the phenomenon of linguistic underdevelopment. The post-independence constitution of each of these countries explicitly affirms that Arabic is the national official language. Yet, the special use of French (spoken and written) is still a prevailing common phenomenon is these societies particularly in the various modern sectors. One manifestation of linguistic underdevelopment is the wide spread of the franco-arabe (spoken Arabic mixed with spoken French) nearly among all groups of today's Maghrebian societies (Dhaouadi 1996: 107-125). National government policies of Arabization have not yet been entirely able to promote the status of Arabic to a fully used language (spoken and written) in all sectors of these nations. As such, the societies of North Africa suffer, though to a considerable lesser degree, like the majority of Black African societies from linguistic underdevelopment. However, Algeria, Tunisia and Morocco have, on the whole, a much better chance than the rest of the African states in ending linguistic underdevelopment. This is for the following reasons:

First, Arabic is spoken and understood by the vast majority of the entire population of these three countries. Second, Arabic is the sacred language of the Holly Book (The Qu'ran) of the Islamic faith to which adhere the Arabs and the Berbers of the Maghreb. Third, as a language, Arabic is a fully articulated and sophisticated language to be able to adapt itself to modern changes. It had already proved its great vitality during the Golden Age of Arab-Muslim civilization. The enormous movement of translation undertaken by this civilization, especially under the Califa El Maamun's rule, illustrates very well the capacity of the Arabic language in intergreating Greek philosophy, Persian and Indian sciences and wisdom into the Arabic-Islamic-culturo-scientific heritage which Europe had greatly benefited from. Based on this, the relative linguistic underdevelopment of Arabic in Algeria, Tunisia and Morocco has mainly resulted from *the French linguistic and cultural colonization* and not from inherent linguistic handicaps which afflict Black Africa as referred to earlier.

Thus, successful Arabisation becomes here the key for dealing with linguistic underdevelopment. However, social policies, enthusiasm and determination of the post-independence regimes in those countries have not unanimously[2] been in favour of Arabization. The general weak and ambivalent attitude of political authorities toward Arabization particulary in Tunisia and Morocco has contributed, since independence in 1956, to the delay of the linguistic underdevelopment eradication in these independent countries inspite of the Arabic language's great potentialities for promotion and advancement.

c) Linguistic underdevelopment in Asia and Central America:

The case of linguistic underdevelopment in Africa presented here is far from being confined only to this continent. Linguistic underdevelopment is found as well in Asia and the Central American countries where particularity English and French imperialism have ruled. English as the official or semi-official language in India and Pakistan has created foundations for the development of linguistic underdevelopment of the Hindi or the Urdu language, so has the use of French in the state of Haiti with its similar implications on native languages and dialects. [3]

2) Third World's underdevelopment in modern sciences and knowledge

Two Manifestations are used here as indexes of Third World's underdevelopment in modern science and knowledge:

- Developing countries' acute dependency on Western science and knowledge (Alatas, F., 2003: 599-613).
- The Third Worlds' scientists, intellectuals… of Western education background often have poor knowledge of their own civilization and cultures' past contributions into the fields of science and knowledge (Alatas, S., 2006 : 7-23).

a) Western monopoly in modern science and knowledge:

There is no question that today's Western advanced societies have an overall monopoly on modern science and knowledge (Mendelson 1976). In the contemporary period, the Third World has not been only dependent on the West in the fields of exact sciences such as physics, medicine, biology, computer sciences, etc… but as well in the corpus of the social sciences like sociology, economics, political science, psychology, etc… This is another feature of the OU as seen through my concept of HS (Dahouadi 2000: 39-64).

b) Third World's past contribution in science/knowledge and its present dependency on the West:

This does not mean, however, that non-Western civilizations had no recorded contributions in science and knowledge. Chinese, Indian, Persian and Arab-Muslim civilizations are known for their significant accumulated heritage of knowledge and science. European contact late in the Middle Ages with Muslim centres of sciences and knowledge especially in Spain and Sicily is considered by many as the triggering spark of Western European Renaissance which had set the scene for the Western great achievements in modern times in science and knowledge (Nasr 1992). Underdeveloped societies' actual heavy dependency on Western science and knowledge may be seen as a very damaging handicap that blocks their capacities to exploit their potentialities and self-develop themselves. History shows that human societies can hardly aspire for continuous progress and development without good standing in scientific and knowledge achievements. Science and knowledge play a similar role to that of the natural selection as far as the survival and the progress of human societies. The more science and knowledge they have, the more adaptation and exploitation societies can make to their environment. It is because of this that an increasing number of experts see *the real gap* which separates the developed from the underdeveloped nations lies in the domains of science and knowledge and not only in the differences in economic growth rates. Thus, winning the battle against underdevelopment and catching up with the advanced countries becomes a hopeless target for today's Third World countries without *the self-mastery of science and knowledge*. The transfer of Western science and knowledge to developing nations can hardly be the alternative to self-development of science and knowledge in the Third World.

c) The shortsightness of Western vision in sciences/ knowledge:

Furthermore, Third World's self-creative processes in science and knowledge do not mean that the developing countries must blindly abide by Western modern vision in these vital fields. Because the nature of human science and knowledge is far from being free from the influences of the history, the socio-economic conditions, the cultural value systems etc. ...of a given society or civilization. Thus, the forces which have shaped the modern outlook of Western science and knowledge are not necessarily the same forces which may or should affect the Third World's ethics and visions of its new self-developed science and knowledge. Arab-Muslim civilization's philosophy, vision and practice of science and knowledge may be cited as an illustration of this difference from Western civilization. Islamic science and knowledge differ in their epistemological/ethical premises and practices from their Western counterparts. This can be shown in the following five points of comparison.

d) The ethics of Western sciences/ knowledge:

1. The Promotheous principle: conflict between Man and God over the possession of knowledge.
2. Promotheous' struggle for knowledge is humanly centered. That is, human use of that knowledge is either indifferent or hostile to non-humans. God's existence, presence etc. ...is outrightly denied or marginalized and Nature is considered an enemy. So it has to be conquered and mastered. This is the result of the Greek egoistic human centered vision of the world (Mendelsohn 1976).
3. Because the Promotheous inspired knowledge is human centered, its negative impact on non-human elements of the universe is to be expected in the relation with Nature as well as with humans as shown in Western colonialism and imperialism.

4. Promotheous human self-centereness has led, still, in the West to a greater narrowness of the notion of humanity. Promotheous based Western science and knowledge's ethics has in the last centuries privileged fewer selected groups of nations while exploited at large many more others of the same human race.

5. Modern Western science and knowledge have restricted their sources to the tangible sense data. They are uni-dimensional (materialistic) in nature. In doing so, they have become hostile or, at best, indifferent, to divine revelation, spiritualism as source of information for the making of human science and knowledge (Randall 1976: 208-209, Landan 1976).

e) The ethics of Islamic science/knowledge:

1. No conflict exists between Man and Allah. The Qu'ran, for instance, overencourages Man to learn through science and knowledge. But Allah's knowledge is infinite while Man's is always limited (you have been granted very little of (real) knowledge: The Qu'ran: 17/85).

2. All creatures of the universe are Allah's. A firm belief in Him and a devoted worship imply a conscious and a categorical respect for Allah's all creatures including Nature. The outcome is the establishment of an ever conscious awareness of the intimate interrelations that tie all the world's phenomena together. The consequence of this is a total respect by scientists for the subjects and objects of their studies.

3. The deep global moral religious world vision of the Muslim scientist or scholar is expected to stand very strongly against the harming of Allah's all creatures.

4. Because all humans are equal before Allah, Islamic science/knowledge's ethics can tolerate neither exploitation nor discrimination against other humans because of their color, genes, ethnic origin, etc. ..

5. Islamic science and knowledge rely on two sources. On the one hand, there is the sense data source, on the other, there is the extra sense data source symbolized particularly in divine revelations and personality traits of scientists (Hunt 1982: 284). Thus, the Islamic base of science and knowledge is dual-dimensional. In Arabic terms, *the Muslim mind is a cognitive Aql-Naql mind.* That is, it uses both human reasoning and revelation in the building of the corpus of science and knowledge. Ibn Khaldun (1332-1406), the first sociologist in the world's intellectual history, was strongly Aql-Naql mind scholar (Dhaouadi 2005: 585-591).

f) Third World's major obstacles to self-developed sciences/ knowledge:

The widespread of the monopoly of Western science and knowledge in the Third World has been consolidated by the colonial educational system which was put in place by the colonizing power in these countries. As we have seen, English and French imperialisms had not only spread in their colonies their languages but they had as well exposed the natives, those who went to school, to the ethics and the practice of Western science and knowledge. The result of this educational acculturation has led to the emergence of Western educated groups[4] who have a poor or distorted knowledge of their own civilization's cultural heritage in the domains of science and knowledge. Algerian, Tunisian and Moroccan scientists, intellectuals...of French academic background can be cited as an example. With their general ignorance, on the one hand, of the Arab-Muslim civilization's contribution in science and knowledge and, on the other, with their French training in Western science and knowledge they become themselves a sort of an *internal system* capable, because of its power, of diffusing Western vision, philosophy and practices of science and knowledge in their own societies. The widespread of this cultural infrastructure is bound to keep Third World's heavy dependency on Western science and knowledge for a long time to come and, thus, hampers those countries from becoming self-creative and self-productive and self-assertive in these crucial domains (Alatas, F., 2003 : 599-613).

g) Self-made sciences /knowledge's role in development:

Without the self-creative process in science and knowledge taking place, both the independence and the future of development and growth in developing societies are (and will be) seriously compromised. Self-development in science and knowledge is of fundamental importance for human societies to achieve maturity and self-managing capacities.

Self-made science and knowledge are essential acquisitions for society's authentic self-dynamism. The self-innovation and use of science and knowledge make the latter more relevant and valid to society's use. With this, society can help itself consolidate its own autonomy and, thus, put itself in a firm standing for reliable and continuing development and growth.

Being dominated by the West in recent history, Third World nations tend to be greater imitators in many fields of their superior (Ibn Khaldoun 1974: 116). The domains of science and knowledge are no exception. Western educated elites of underdeveloped societies are unlikely to take serious critical stand of certain aspects of Western outlook of science and knowledge. This attitude should be no surprise at all. On the one hand, their educational acculturation process into the vision, the philosophy and the practices of Western science and knowledge leaves *little room for dissent or criticism*. On the other hand, their poor or distorted knowledge of their civilization's heritage in science and knowledge can hardly enable them to formulate or seek to establish new alternatives to the philosophy and ethics of modern Western science and knowledge. Contrary to this general apathetic position of Third World scientists, intellectuals… the number of intellectual and scientific publications on the crises of knowledge, in the West, has been on the increase in recent years (Boudon 1984, Wallersein 2001). Questions are addressed to the epistemology, the materialism, the coherence, the ethics, etc… of modern science and knowledge.

Thus, grasping non-Western civilization's outlook on these critical issues of modern science and knowledge would certainly initiate Third World scientists, scholars, etc… to undertake *the indigenization process* of social and human sciences in their own countries. With this, the scene will be set for the undermining of developing nations' underdevelopment in those sciences and other branches of science and knowledge.

3) Third World's underdevelopment in cultural values system

a) The general and subtle rule of cultural exchanges:

The contact, in modern times, between the dominant West and the dominated Third World has enabled the former to impose the spread of its own cultural values, particularly those of modernity in the underdeveloped societies. The phenomenon of the Westernization of Third World customs and morals is largely a result of this type of balance of power between the two parties (Inquiry Magazine 1985). This is in line with the spirit of a quasi-universal law which tends to regulate the nature of the process of cultural exchanges during human civilizations' encounters. This law stipulates that the weaker the conquered, the dominated, the subordinate, …) is often inclined to imitate more or less the stronger (the conqueror, the dominant, the superior, …). Ibn Khaldoun, the famous Arab historian-sociologist of the Middle Ages, had explicitly stated the principles of who imitates whom in his Muqaddimah (Ibn Khaldoun 1974: 116). Contemporary social science research literature disagrees only in certain nuances with the author of the Muqaddimah on this point (Devos 1976: 5). For instance, the diffusion of Western cultural value system in developing societies is a fact which can't be denied. However, the nature and the degree of this cultural diffusion is far from being uniform among the different social groups of Third World countries. On the one side, groups of Western education background as well as urban citizens are more likely to be more exposed and, thus, affected by the spread of Western cultural values. On the other, the illiterate as well as non-urban population of the Third World is understandably the least influenced by Western culture. Furthermore, Western acculturation to urban residents and those groups of Western educational training has no identical impact on all dimensions of the acculturation process. While French language is a widespread linguistic feature in today's Algeria, Tunisia and Morocco, Christian religious values have hardly had any sympathy among those Muslim groups during the French colonization. The cultural exchange process between people has, therefore, its own subtleties and nuances. In cultural matters, it is not only the dominant party's sheer superiority which dictates what the dominated party will adopt from the culture of his superior. This is true not only of the interaction of the North African culture with its French counterpart in modern times, but also of other previous cultural encounters between civilizations. Though the Arab Muslims were the dominant power in the Middleeast in the earlier spread of Islam they were not able, however, to spread evenly Arabic and the Islamic values (as HS components) among the population they had ruled. While Arabic has become the language of the area called today the Arab World, Christianity has survived among significant minorities in many Arab societies . Persian civilization's encounter with Islam had resulted in a different cultural exchange pattern. The majority of Persians had adopted Islam (Shia Islam) as their new faith while the adoption of the Arabic language has remained very limited in this new land of Islam.

b) Western cultural disorganizing effect in the Third World

Third World's contact with the dominant modern West in contemporary times has led to some erosion, disorganisation in its own cultural values system. Modern Western cultural values have their greatest impact, as pointed out earlier, on those groups of western background education and residents of urban centres. But even among the most Westernized of these groups complete Western acculturation has hardly ever occurred. In many cases Western cultural values never took root in the infrastructure of the cultural values system of the Third World countries. They have *remained superficial* because of their self-imposed nature on those societies. A scholar like Ali Mazuri sees that one of the greatest dilemma of today's Africa is "a dialect consequence of the fact that its institutions and ideologies are alien lacking any African roots whatsoever" (Mazuri 1980). Political instability and widespread authoritarianism in the Black, continent are considered by Mazuri as a result of cultural disorganization which has been brought about mainly by Western colonialism in modern times.

What is at stake here is the clash between tradition (Third World cultures) and modernity (the new cultural values and visions of Western civilization since the 19th century). This is a theme which is often covered with ethnocentrism by contemporary Western sociologists. Most of their studies don't hesitate to side ideologically with modernity (Westernization) against tradition (non-Western cultures) (Lerner 1964). Post-colonial Tunisia can be cited as an example to make the point stressed here.

c) Tradition/modernization's impact on Tunisian society:

Tunisia's attempts to modernize (to Westernize) since independence (1956), under Bourguiba's pro-Western leadership, have probably led it to undergo the most acute linguistico-cultural values conflict compared to its neighbours Algeria and Morocco. Modern Western outlook on alcoholic drinking, sexuality and women's equality/freedom is bound to clash more and less with the Tunisian Islamic-Arabic Mediterranean cultural value system. This dualistic culture heritage can often lead to what modern social scientists have called anomie, cultural disorganization/ confusion and tension.[5]

This situation can hardly help the Tunisians consolidate their cultural identity or promote their own cultural values system. Such a critical cultural confusion is a principal source for the hardening of culture-symbolic under-development as defined in this chapter. Furthermore, Westernization has practically taken over especially among *the younger Tunisian generations* in the area of dress. Wearing Western dress for young Tunisians rarely consti-tutes any conscious feeling of internal conflict. In other words, wearing tradi-tional clothing is no longer a real alternative to the self-imposed Western one. Western dress for them is, therefore, a fait accompli. This does not mean, however, that modern and modernizing Tunisians don't wear any more their traditional dress. They do but in a ritual manner. That is, on special occasions. During the summer, a great number of men dress up in Jubba (a long outer garment).

At wedding or circumcision celebrations Tunisian modern women may be seen in traditional or semi-traditional clothing. Thus, as a cultural heritage, the traditional Tunisian dress has been seriously marginalized. As such, it is another feature of *cultural underdevelopment* in this North African country. In brief, the three categories of cultural underdevelopment discussed in this section, represent on the whole an impoverishment/a disruption/disorganiza-tion of these main cultural-symbolic (language, science/knowledge and the cultural values system) of the cultures of the New Nations.

THE PSYCHOLOGICAL UNDERDEVELOPMENT IN THE THIRD WORLD

a) The definition of psychological underdevelopment:

Psychological underdevelopment is used here to mean the deterioration of the basic foundations of the psychological well being of the personality of the individual of the Third World as a result especially of contemporary Western imperial culturo-symbolic domination. Syndromes like loss of faith in one's self, strong desire to imitate the Other (The West), spread of inferior-ity complex, feeling of alienation are considered to be possible symptoms of his psychological underdevelopment' in today's developing societies.

b) Culturo-symbolic domination and deterioration of self- esteem:

The three aspects of the culture-symbolic underdevelopment just outlined make it clear that *Western colonialism and imperialism* of the 19th and 20th century in the Third World has not been limited to military, economic and political domination. But it has been as well *a culturo-symbolic*. Some of today's developing countries had experienced total Western domination under Western colonialism. The French style of occupation of Algeria is a case in point. This interaction between the two parties has often led, on the one hand, to the development of *inferiority complex symptoms* among dominated people of the Third World and, on the other, to the development of superiority complex among the Western dominant societies. Western culturo-symbolic domination in its two forms 1 and 2 spelled out earlier has shown its detrimental effects on the self-esteem of the culture-symbolic dominated individual of underdeveloped countries. French colonial culture-symbolic domination of the North African societies is an example. The French had made serious attempts to *de-culturalize* the North Africans from their Arabic-Islamic heritage and acculturalize them instead to the French language and its culture. The result of this process has been the creation of culturo-symbolic inferiority complex among Algerians, Tunisians and Moroccans who have had a predominant French education, as pointed out. On the one side, these Maghrebians[6] have had high admiration for the French language and culture. Their widely and frequent use of French[7] is a good indicator of their *compulsive attachment* to the French culture in general (Dhaouadi 1996: 107-125). On the other hand, they are found to consider Arabic and its culture as traditional (outdated) and, thus, unsuitable for modernity (Westernization). Their acculturation into the dominant French culture has made them *feel uneasy with regard to their relations with the Arabic language and its culture.* Knowing one's language and culture becomes, therefore, a source of feeling inferior instead of feeling proud as usually occurs under normal circumstances (Dhaouadi 2002).

c) Inferiority complex and linguistic avoidance response

This has developed among this type of educated North Africans, what I may call *a Linguistic Avoidance-Response* phenomenon vis-à-vis Arabic.

In Tunisia, for instance, it has been repeatedly observed by this author even among the post-independence generation of students of high school as well as of university that they tend to use, while speaking in Tunisian dialect the term "L'arabe" (Arabic) in French instead of "al- arabiyya" when refering to the course of Arabic language. Avoiding using Arabic is well conveyed by the example of these Tunisian students. So is their admiration for the use of French even when speaking about Arabic!

The connotations of this linguistic behavior suggest that these *Tunisians are hardly proud of Arabic* as their national language. The negative image they have held of Arabic from colonial and postcolonial times is bound to be, to a large degree, *the outcome of French colonial hostile ideology toward Arabic and its culture.* The phenomenon of Linguistic Avoidance-Response is symptomatic of a psycho-cultural crisis. On the cultural side, French culture-symbolic acculturation of these Tunisian students appears to be overwhelming and, thus, their alienation from their culture-symbolic heritage (Arabic language and its culture) is quite visible. On the psychological side, there is a deterioration to one's self- esteem, one's faith in one's identity, etc... (psychological underdevelopment 1). In other words, the psychological dimensions of *the Basic Personality* of those Tunisians are somewhat eroded and undermined. In short, what is involved here are (1) the development of false (distorted) culturo-symbolic identities and (2) The appearance of manifest syndromes of inferiority complex.

d) Cultural values system and disorganized personality:

The acute state of cultural conflicts between the traditional cultural values system and its modern Western counterparts is expected to have certain side effects on the personality structure of the Third World acculturized (to Western culture) individual. Some modern sociologists have referred to this type of personality as "disorganized personality" .Psychological Underdevelopment 2), (Znaniecki, Thomas 1958). This disorganization of the cultural values system (Cultural Underdevelopment 3) is often associated in human societies by socio-behavioral manifestations such as social tension. protest, socio-cultural change, deviance and crime rise and increase in mental illness (Kisker, 1982: 103-106). The latter is accounted for by the fact that cultural values conflicts expose the person to psychological strains, stress and tension due to the adjustment he or she has to make to the polarizing nature of his/her cultural values system. As seen, the self-imposed Western cultural values have practically intruded more or less all Third World societies. The study of the confrontation between the two cultural values systems and their implications constitute a potential rich area of social science research yet to be fully explored especially by Third World social scientists (Dhaouadi : 2002). In putting their efforts in this new vista of research, Third World social scientists will unravel in a more systematic and scientific manner not only the nature and the variety of the psycho-cultural impacts on underdeveloped countries but they will as well push forward *the social sciences indigenization process* in their own societies (Alatas 2006 : 7-23).

THE OTHER UNDERDEVELOPMENT AS A PSYCHO-CULTURAL SYSTEM

As shown throughout this chapter, the Other Underdevelopment appears to be a phenomenon of psycho-cultural nature. Its two components are mutually interacting in a reciprocal manner. We have seen, on the one hand, that linguistic underdevelopment (1) and science/knowledge underdevelopment (2) are likely to lead to the development of inferiority complex symptoms (Psychological Underdevelopment 1) in the personality of the Westernly acculturized individual of the Third World. On the other, psychological underdevelopment predisposes the individual's personality with more readiness as well as with motivation to learn and use the language(s) and the culture(s) of dominant societies. Furthermore, the inferiority complex becomes a strong force causing the development of a negative perception of one's national language and culture.

Psychological inferiority complex symptoms (Psychological Underdevelopment 1) appear, thus, to harden the two dimensions (1 & 2) of cultural underdevelopment and consequently, contribute to the making of cultural alienation, a phenomenon which is widespread in underdeveloped countries especially among those groups of Western education background. All this helps create a state of illiteracy of the Other Underdevelopment particularly among the latter groups. What I have called *disorganised personality* (Psychological Underdevelopment 3) contributes, in turn, to the level of cultural values breakdown (Cultural Underdevelopment). In other words, cultural values conflicts are likely to make the personality structure of the individual of the Third World more vulnerable to further breakdowns and, thus, more receptive or less resistant to the adoption of Western cultural values. All this would tend to lead to deeper desintegration of the personality structure and, consequently, to *confusion in one's cultural identity*. Table 8.1 illustrates the main components of the phenomenon of the Other Underdevelopment as well as the nature of their interaction:

THE ROOTS OF WESTERN MODERN SOCIAL SCIENCES' SILENCE ON THE OU

It must be clear by now that the existence of the Other Underdevelopment phenomenon in the Third World is not based on mere speculation or imagination. We have defined the Other Undevelopment and spelled out its psycho-cultural components which convey its very nature. However, Western (Liberal Capitalist or Socialist Marxist) modern social sciences have remained in general silent as far as the Other Underdevelopment is con-

Table 8.1. The psycho-cultural nature of the phenomenon of the Other Underdevelopment in the Third World

The components of psychological underdevelopment	1. Third World inferiority complex symptoms toward the dominant West	1. Linguistic underdevelopment	The components of cultural underdevelopment
		2. Underdevelopment in modern science and knowledge	
	2. Disorganized personality and abnormal behavioural and mental symptoms.	3. Cultural values system disorganization	

cerned. Most Third World social scientists have also followed suite (Alatas 2003: 599-613). This silence, as we stated at the outset of this study, requires an explanation: The assessment we offer below would account, in our opinion, for modern Western social scientists mute negligence of the study of the psycho-cultural underdevelopment in the Third World. The causes of that can be classified into two categories:

a) Causes of Western ethnocentric nature:

(1) There is a general widespread attitude, particularly among Western Liberal social scientists, concerned with the study of development/underdevelopment which hints or claims implicitly or explicitly that the cultural heritage (values, traditions, religions. ..) of underdeveloped societies is largely an obstacle to the development process in those countries. This should explain why cultural underdevelopment as defined by us, has no place in their studies of development/underdevelopment in the Third World.

(2) Western ethnocentric vision of development/ underdevelopment has made modern specialists and researchers of the social sciences tend to think that Third World countries can't achieve development on their own. Thus, Third World dependency on external help (preferably Western in nature) is recommended by them. The spread, therefore, of modern Western languages (English, French...) and cultural values into Third World societies is expected to be endorsed or even encouraged especially by Modernization western social scientists (Lerner, 1964, Inkeles and Smith 1974). For the latter it is quite obvious that Western cultural values diffusion in underdeveloped countries is a process which helps the promotion of cultural development and not a process, which leads to the Other Underdevelopment, as we have outlined that in this chapter.

(3) Western Liberal capitalist social scientists have hardly made any link between the phenomenon of underdevelopment in the Third World and Western colonialism of the latter (Ibid). When underdevelopment in all its forms (economic. social, psycho- cultural, etc...) is not related somehow to imperial Western classical or new colonialism in the last two centuries, then the Other Underdevelopment, seen by us as resulting largely from Western domination of the Third World, is unlikely to be recognized and, subsequently, studied by those social scientists.

(4) Western social scientists' conceptualization, understanding, theories, etc... of development/ underdevelopment are bound to be westerncentric. This is only natural. The social scientist, whatever his/her nationality may be, is inclined to rely heavily on the realities of his/her own social/civilizational milieu in analyzing social phenomena as well as theorizing about them. In doing so. it is difficult for him/her not to be, at least partially, biast in going about his/her research endeavours including his/her own, choice of what phenomenon to study. Western social scientists' negligence of the study of the Other Underdevelopment is a case in point. In other words, Western

Capitalist and Socialist advanced societies, to which belong most modern social scientists, are not known to have suffered seriously , if at all, from the Other Underdevelopment syndrome as described in this work. Thus, the Other Underdevelopment has remained an alien phenomenon which has failed to attract seriously their scientific curiosity.

b) Causes of epistemological nature:

1. Generally speaking Western Liberal as well as Marxist social scientists, conceptualization of the development/phenomena is materialistic in nature. If development/ underdevelopment is conceived basically in terms of economic, social, scientific and technological indicators, then it becomes understandable why the psycho-cultural underdevelopment has drawn little or no attention at all from those social scientists. It is well known that Marxist social thinkers (Baran,1960) have over spoken about Third World economic exploitation by the Capitalist West but they have given not more than a lip service to Third World cultural exploitation.

2. As pointed out, The Other Underdevelopment constitutes an underdevelopment which focuses mainly on the factors leading to the deterioration (the underdevelopment) of the psycho-cultural components of the individual's personality in the Third World. Thus, the psycho-cultural underdevelopment is not materialistic *in* nature. If development/underdevelopment is conceived by Western social scientists, primarily in terms of structural-materialistic variables, then the whole issue of the Other Underdevelopment can hardly find any attention among structuralist-materialistic social scientists. By neglecting to study the Other Underdevelopment as an essential compelling feature of Third World societies, modern Western sociologists and economists in particular have put into serious question the integrity as well as the validity of their own paradigms and theories about development/ underdevelopment in the Third World.

REFERENCES

Alatas, S., H. (2006). The Autonomous, the Universal and the Future of Sociology. *Current Sociology, 54*(1).

Alatas, S., F. (2003). Academic Dependency and the Global Division of Labour in the Social Sciences. *Current Sociology, 51*(6), 599-613.

Baran. (1960). *The Political Economy of Growth.* New York: Mentor.

Bauman, Z. (2000). *Liquid Modernity.* Cambridge (UK): Polity Press.

Boudon, R. (1984). *La place du désordre.* Paris: PUF.

Devos, G. (1976). *Responses to Change: Culture and Personality.* New York: D. Van Nostrand Company.

Dhaouadi, M. (2005). The Ibar/Lessons of Ibn Khaldoun's Umran Mind. *Contemporary Sociology, 34*(6).

Dhaouadi, M. (2002). *Globalization of the Other Underdevelopment: Third World Culural Identities.* Kuala Lumpur: A.S. Noordeeen.

Dhaouadi, M. (2000). Capitalism's Impending Dangers for Global Humane Development. *American Journal of Islamic Social Sciences, 17*(1).

Dhaouadi, M. (1996). Un essai de théorisation sur le penchant vers l'accent parisien chez la femme tunisienne. *International Journal of the Sociology of Language, 122.*

Frags, K.L. (1984). *Encyclopedic Atlas of the World.* London: Apple Press Ltd.

Hunt, M. (1982). *The Universe Within : A New Science Explores The Human Mind.* New York: Simon and Schuster.

Khaldun, Ibn. (1974). *The Muqaddimah: An Introduction to History.* Dawood, N.J. (Ed.). (Franz Rosenthal, Trans.). Princeton Bolling Series: Princeton University Press.

Inkeles, E. and Smith, D. (1974). *Becoming Modern.* Cambridge, MA: Harvard University Press.

When Cultures Meet… (1985). *Inquiry Magazine, 2*(6).

Jacquemot, P. (1981). *Economie et sociologie du tiers-monde : guide bibliographique.* Paris: L'Harmattan.

Kister, G. (1982). *The Disorganized Personality.* London: McGraw-Hill Inc.

Landan, P. (1976). *The Arab Heritage of Western Civilization.* New York: Arab Information Center.

Lerner, D. (1964). *The Passing of Traditional Society.* New York: the Free Press.

Mazrui, A. (1980). *The African Condition: The Reith Lectures.* London: Heinemann.

Mendelson, K. (1976). *Science and Western Domination.* London: Thames and Hudson.

Nasr, S.H. (1992). *Science and Civilization in Islam.* New York: Barnes and Noble Books.

Pieterse, J.N. (2001). *Development Theory: Deconstructions / Reconstructions.* London: Sage Publications.

Randall, J.H. (1976). *The Making of the Modern Mind.* New York.

Thomas, W, Znaniecki, F. (1958). *The Polish Peasant in Europe and America.* New York: Dover Publications, Inc.

Wallerstein, I. (2001). *Unthinking Social Science.* Temple: Temple University Press.

Wurn, S. (2001). *Atlas of the World's Languages in Danger of Disappearing.* Paris: UNESCO.

NOTES

1. Fanon is probably the only Third World intellectual who had written with clarity and depth about the psycho-cultural scars, caused by Western Imperialism, to the personality of the dominated people of the Third World. He had referred to French policy which attempted to alienate the Algerian from his own language(s) and culture and reduce him to a state of absolute de-personalization. The Algerian was a victim of an abortive attempt to de-culturalize him. For him as for us, colonialism is a global phenomenon including an psycho-cultural dimensions. To undo colonialism, Third World nations must eradicate the manifestations of the OU. For Fanon, the process of de-colonization is not only national in form, it is violent in content. See his books:1.Black Skin, White Masks/New York, Grove Press,1967.2.The Wretched of the Earth/ Présence Africaine, London, 1963.
Our effort here is to systematize and make the phenomenon of the OU measurable by concrete reliable indicators. In doing so, we are hoping to dissipate all vagueness which may have been one of the excuses used by some social scientists, in order not to put the phenomenon of the OU under rigorous scrutiny.

2. The first president of Tunisia (1956-1987) after independence, Habib Bourguiba, was strongly in favour of the continuing wide of the French language in Tunisian society. He and his regime appeared to consider French linguistic and cultural colonization as a positive dimension of French colonialism. This is compatible with the French Law of February 2005 which speaks about "*le rôle positif*" colonialism. The consequence of this can be felt and seen in the weak attitude of Tunisians towards Arabic (their national language) after 50 years of independence (2006). Today, the Arabic language has no first position in their hearts or in their minds or in their daily usages.

3. Westerners often form their wrong impressions about Third World educated men and women of Western education background. This is more true of North Americans. In their encounter particularly with Third World students in their countries Americans and Canadians are frequently impressed by those foreign students' fluency in English or French (or both).

 Chapter 8

Their amazement becomes stronger when they believe that those students must know and master better their own languages. In many cases this perception is entirely false. Had they been aware of linguistic underdevelopment in the Third World, as described here they would have avoided being naive about the nature of Western domination and its global impact on dominated peoples.

4. They are often those who have more power in running their countries after independence. Groups of traditional education have hardly had much power in Third World societies since independence. The indigenization process of human and social sciences in these countries remains difficult to achieve in these circumstances. Attempts to islamise those sciences carried out by the late great Muslim thinker Ismail AI Faruqui and the Institute of Islamic Thought (IIIT,Washington Dc) are far from being, in our opinion, the natural solution to the self-development of authentic Islamic human and social science and knowledge. The real Islamization of knowledge can really take place only when it is initiated and self-developed by Muslim scientists, intellectuals... whose socio-cultural milieu and ethics are Islamic in nature. See (1) Islamization of Knowledge: General Principles and Work Plan by 1. Al-Faruqi (IIIT, Washington 1982), and (2)"Islamizing the Behavioral Sciences" in Enquiry Magazine, Vol. 3, No.7, London, July 1986. pp. 54-58.

5. Summer 1986 has witnessed several manifestations of tensions political disarry in Tunisia. President Bourguiba's dismissal of his prime minister M. M'Zali and a number of his ministers is linked partially to M'Zali sympathetic attitude toward the Tunisian Islamist Movement. Members of this movement were executed by Bourguiba pro-Western regime. The conflict between traditional Islamic values and modern Adopted Western ones appears to be one important factor for this political tension at the highest level in Tunisia, in Bourguiba's era and shortly after Ben Ali took over.

6. Maghrebians=Algerians, Tunisians and Moroccans. The word Maghreb englobes, therefore, the three countries: Algeria, Tunisia and Morocco.

7. The frequent French use in these countries takes essentially two forms:
a) The widespread exclusive of French is common particularly among educated groups of French training where dealing with modern scientific, intellectual... subjects.
b) The Franco-Arabe (mixing Arabic with French in speaking) is much more spread among the general population of these three societies. North African educated women, in particular, appear to over mix their Arabic with French more than their Maghrebian counterparts.

Chapter Nine

The Arab Muslim World Set to Dialogue with the West: A Cultural Perspective

THE CHAPTER THESIS

I would like to argue in this chapter that the West is less predisposed than the Arab Muslim world for civilizations dialogue (Dhaouadi 2005:8-15). Consequently, the West may be considered as the major source of Huntington's so called 'Clash of Civilizations'. My observation is largely different from Huntington's set of ideas (Huntington 1993). On the one hand, my thesis is based on the assumptions that common cultures (languages, religious beliefs, cultural values...= *HS*) between peoples, societies, nations are essential factors that encourage and facilitate contacts and dialogues between peoples and civilizations. On the other hand, the lack or the absence of common HS between humans would discourage and hamper contacts and dialogues and, subsequently, create conditions which may favour tensions, clashes and conflicts between them. I will explain in this chapter how the widespread knowledge of western languages, Christian beliefs and western knowledge/science cultural values system among the large population of the Arab Muslim world motivate Arabs and Muslims to desire to have contact and dialogue with Westerners and their civilization.

THE HS THEORY

The above thesis on the importance of these shared HS elements for civilizations 'dialogue is based on Basic Research observations and findings. The latter, as seen in previous chapters, have made me strongly claim that 'humans are by nature cultural symbolic beings'. That is, HS represent the core of the identities of the human individuals and their societies and civilisations. I reached this conclusion as a result of the following explanations and arguments.

The words 'human symbolic' derive from the terms "Human Symbols" (HS) which mean, as already well known in this book's chapters, all those distinctive human symbolic traits: spoken and written language, thought, religion, knowledge / science, myths, laws, cultural values and norms. My analysis of the HS system had made me realize that *language is the Mother of all HS*, as stressed before. This would imply that none of the remaining HS can really exist without the prior existence of human language in its spoken forms, at least. In other words, human language is the single most important source for the emergence of the phenomenon of human culture /HS as pointed out in the first chapter of this work. (Dhaouadi 2006).

HS AND CULTURES DIALOGUE

The elaboration of the HS theory helps put the issue of civilisations dialogue or clash into perspective. First, based on the centrality of HS in the human identity it is more appropriate to use the term culture instead of civilization in the analysis of the issue of dialogue between today peoples, societies and civilizations. This is, because culture is, on the one hand, the basic founding element of a given civilization and, on the other hand, it is the decisive force, as already explained repeatedly, in determining and encouraging the dialogue process or vice versa between humans. So it is more accurate to speak of *cultures dialogues* rather than civilizations dialogues.

Since the end of the 20th century many books and articles have been published on this subject as well as numerous seminars, colloquium and congresses have been held in different parts of the world.

The success of the project of civilizations dialogue could hardly crystallize and be fruitful without the dialogue of the cultures of human civilizations. Because cultures/HS represent the core of the identities of human individuals and their societies and civilisations, as stressed above in the argument of my HS theory.

Given that languages are, according to the assumptions of the HS theory, the essential creating forces of the phenomenon of human cultures, it becomes very appropriate to consider peoples' learning of each other languages as a practical and *effective green visas* that facilitates the process of dialogue between the concerned parties whose civilisations wish to dialogue (Bochner 1985:99-126)

However, today western advanced societies and developing countries *are not equal* on the learning scale of each other languages. On the one hand, at least some large social groups from the South (the Third World countries) know fairly well some of the languages of the Western developed countries. English and French are the most widely spread known and used Western languages in the Third World. On the other hand, all social groups and classes of Western advanced societies do not have even a limited knowledge of the Third World's languages.

This situation is true of the state of dialogue between the Western world and the Arab Muslim world. Calls in favour of such a dialogue are getting stronger especially since September 11, 2001. From the point of view of my HS theory, the West is less ready and skilled linguistically and, thus, culturally to get into a serious and wide dialogue with the Arab Muslim world. Most populations of Western social classes do not know any of the major languages of the Arab Muslim world which are: Arabic, Persian, Turkish and Urdu. This situation leads, consequently, to the widespread Western ignorance of the cultures of the Arab Muslim societies (Bochner 1985:5-44,81-98) .This could hardly encourage and enable the West for a wide grass root dialogue with the Arab Muslim world.

In this regard, Americans may be considered - in linguistic and cultural terms- less predisposed for dialogue with other cultures. Because they are, for instance, more handicapped by their wide spread ignorance of foreign languages than most of the advanced European Western societies. In my own terms, they are massively illiterate of foreign language(s) as green visa tool that could solicit them to like to enter into dialogue with others. This may be one of the reasons which may explain, for instance, why the slogan of Clash of Civilizations has come from the US culture and not from the European one.

In contrast to that, there is in the Arab and Muslim societies a wide genuine knowledge of Western cultures because of the wide spread usage particularly of English and French in those societies during Western colonization and after especially among the elites and the middle and the higher classes of the Arab Muslim population. As such, my HS theory shows that the desire for civilizations dialogue is not equal between the western advanced societies and the Arab Muslim peoples. The greater knowledge of Western languages and cultures among the Arab Muslim population enable them to have greater motivation and aspiration than their western counterparts to strongly welcome and act in favour of the dialogue with the West.

The Arab Muslim world scores also better than the West on *the religious scale knowledge*. On the one hand, Muslims strongly believe in Moses and Jesus as prophets and God's Messengers. The belief in other divine prophets and messengers throughout the ages is a fundamental component of the Muslim faith. Consequently, Christians and Jews are seen by Muslims as the Peoples of the Revealed Books.

On the other hand, Judaism and Christianity do not preach to their followers to believe in Islam and Mohammad as its prophet and Messenger.

In other words, the West shows *great ignorance* of the Arab Muslim world's languages, religions and cultures. Social psychologists would strongly point out that ignorance of other peoples cultures constitute a major source for the display of *prejudices, stereotyped attitudes and widespread false accusations of them* (Bochner 1985:5-44).

Furthermore, the West remains today the dominant power in this world. Certainly, these two factors have the tendency to reinforce each other in order to establish, on the one hand, an inferior image of Arabs and Muslims and a superior image of Westerners, on the other hand.

According to my HS theory, the population of the Western world at large has more difficulty linguistically and religiously than its Arab and Muslim counterpart to really engage in a fair grass root dialogue with the Arab and Muslim world. As such, the West is far from being adequately prepared to advocate, in a spontaneous and motivated manner, an open and sincere dialogue with the Arab Muslim world with all respect and equality.

Huntington's thesis does not make mention of the importance of the presence or the absence of linguistic and religious factors in the making of dialogue or Clash of Civilizations. As shown, these factors point out that the Arab Muslim world has greater desire and willingness to engage in dialogue with the Western world.

Furthermore, Huntington's theoretical assumptions display a lot of *prejudice and misunderstanding not only toward the Arab Muslim civilization but toward the Chinese civilization as well.* Such an attitude does not surely help the establishment of credible scientific knowledge and science. Huntington's view lacks full presence of a neutral and objective spirit in advancing his theory of the Clash of Civilizations. Consequently, he can not easily claim to be one of those who really commit themselves to science as their true vocation.

WESTERN SCIENCE'S APPEAL OPENS DIALOGUE WITH THE WEST

In addition to the already mentioned factors inviting Arabs and Muslims alike to welcome dialogue with the Western world, there is also the factor of the West's great advancement and leadership in modern science and knowledge that strongly encourage the Arab Muslim world to stress the major importance of opening the dialogue gate quite wide with the West.

This is not only for pragmatic and beneficial reasons, as the case may be in many developing countries. But, this is due as well to the similarity between Islam and the West in their cultural value systems which consider the promotion of knowledge and science as very central and a first priority in human societies and civilizations. This type of similarity does not only strengthen the desire for dialogue with the West among the Arabs and Muslims, but it may also solicit Western respect for the Arabs Muslims who were pioneers in the development of science and knowledge which is seen by many as the basis for the coming of the European Renaissance. The common praise of knowledge and science by both Islamic and Western cultures will shortly be described below.

With the above underlined numerous positive factors in favour particularly of Arab Muslim dialogue and not Clash with the western world, Huntington's theory of Clash of Civilizations needs to be questioned in its crude application on the Arab Muslim world. The latter, as explained, has many more strong reasons than the West has in favour of dialoguing and not clashing with the West.

HUNTINGTON'S THEORY IN QUESTION

Today, as already shown, there is an international wide use of the theory of Clash of Civilizations in the media, in intellectual circles and even in the common daily life of men and women around the world. The events of September 11, 2001 may have boosted the popularity of this theory particularly in the US.

The debate on the credibility of Huntington's theory is still waging and out of which two main camps could be identified. On the one hand, one camp strongly believes in the importance of the theory especially for the understanding of the West's relation with the Muslim world. On the other hand, the second camp seriously questions the very credibility of Huntington's theory. It is argued, for instance, that the idea of the Clash of Civilizations is the outcome of *a political situation*. It is an attempt to create a new paradigm which replaces the theory of the Cold War between the former Soviet Union and the Western world led by the USA. As such, the thesis of the theory of the Clash of Civilizations can hardly be considered a scientific one. Furthermore, there are those who see Huntington's theory as having *philosophical background* related to the thinking of Thomas Kuhn, Oswald Spengler, Arnold Toynbee and Fernand Braudel. This background may have overstretched the application of the assumptions of this theory to the Arab Muslim civilization whose many present parameters oppose the clash with Western civilization, as pointed out in this chapter (Saadi 2006: 147-161).

THE ISLAMIC EAST AND THE CHRISTIAN WEST COULD DIALOGUE

In order to complete the assessment of the status of Huntington's theory and reduce its general confusing dimensions, I think it is appropriate now to take a closer look at the similarity factor in knowledge/science cultural value systems of both theArab Muslim and Western civilizations mentioned before in order to see how dialogue with the West is heavily asked for by today Arab Muslims because of the multiple factors at work explained here. This is clearly different from the claim of Huntington's theory of Clash of Civilizations. This similarity factor in knowledge/science cultural values systems of Islam and the West is hardly mentioned let alone analysed and discussed in studies of dialogue or clash of civilizations.

I examine here the attitude of both Arab Muslim and Western civilizations with regard to one single important issue for human civilization's progress and dynamics. This should greatly allow a decent evaluation of the degrees of clashes or convergences between these two civilizations. The theme on which to measure the stand of both civilizations is the place of knowledge and science in their cultural value systems.

There is overwhelming evidence that the acquisition of science and knowledge constitutes a central cultural value of modern Western civilization. That explains the West's leadership today in the tremendous science and knowledge explosion. The West's domination of the world scene is not, thus, limited to military and economic matters but it must be extended well beyond that to its superiority in the fields of knowledge and science which are certainly more strategic, in the long run, for the West's continuing domination of the world.

The origins of the West's leadership in these fields began with the clashes between the Church and the Scientists in the late Middle Age in Europe. With the victory of the latter came the Renaissance which strongly pushed forward the cultivation of secular knowledge and science that has become since the guiding ethics of contemporary Western civilization. With the passing of many centuries with science and knowledge experiences and the countless discoveries in natural and social sciences; has developed a general attitude of highly praising learning and education among the populations of the advanced Western societies to the extent that a sort of a sense of curiosity to explore practically every thing in the world has become a widespread attitude among the citizens of those societies. So the whole world/universe is *an open vista for the Western mind*.

The thirst for knowledge and science is also a fundamental feature of Arab Muslim civilization. The roots of that are, however, *the very opposite of Western civilization's*. They are to be traced to the essence of the Islamic faith itself. The search for knowledge and science is a hard core religious value of Islam. The very first words and verses revealed to the prophet Muhammad in the Qur'an leave no doubt about that:" Read in the name of your Lord and Cherisher…*He Who taught the use of the Pen*, taught man that he did not know"(S:96,v:1,4,5).In this first revelation encounter between the Prophet and the Divine, top priority was not given to economics or material issues but rather to reading and the use of the pen as crucial tools/kit for the acquisition of knowledge and science. Modern social psychology's insights greatly help understand *why reading and the use of the pen had to be mentioned to the Prophet before any thing else.* Social psychologists argue that first human impressions have longer lifespan in human memories. So the first divine revelation ought, therefore, to strongly draw Muhammad's attention to the most important thing that humans must acquire and master in this world and must not marginalize it, let alone forget it , to be truly God's vicar. As such, from a social psychology's outlook the extreme divine emphasis and stress in the Qur'an on the acquisition of science and knowledge as first class priority for the good of humans has to be taken as fully intentional and not just an arbitrary thing in the first verse of the Qur'an.

The stand of the two first references of Islam, the Qur'an and the Hadith (the Prophet's sayings and behaviours), on the crucial importance of knowledge and science is so strong and breathtaking. It is estimated that about *one sixth (1/6) of the Qur'an's verses* is directly or indirectly about science and knowledge and their capital role for the improvement of the human destiny. The text of the Qur'an uses the word science to mean both knowledge and science. It uses the derivatives of the latter as well as an adjective and as a verb in the hundreds of its verses related to knowledge and science:"are people who have knowledge/science equal to those who do not have them? "among all people only true scholars/scientists revere God most".

The sayings of the Prophet are in turn in full support of knowledge and science as first class cultural value of the Islamic religion: "seeking knowledge and science is a religious duty for every Muslim", "seek knowledge and science from the cradle to the grave" "seek knowledge and science as far as China" "scientists and scholars are the true inheritors of the prophets". The capital importance of science and knowledge is, therefore, extremely central in the cultural value system of the Islamic faith as fully expressed in these limited verses of the Qur'an and Hadiths. Thus, there is hardly any surprise for the milestones achieved in knowledge and science by Muslim civilization in its golden age. The Canon of Medicine of Avicenna (980-1037) was the standard text in the medieval world including Europe. As to the Muslim philosopher Averroes (1126-98), his rational thinking is seen by many as the preview of the European Renaissance that came centuries later. Ibn Khaldun's sociological thought (1332-1406) in his Muqaddimah was over four centuries ahead of that of August Comte (1798-1857), the founder of contemporary Western sociology. It surpasses Comte's on many levels by the admission of highly credible Western thinkers like A.Toynbee who wrote of Ibn Khaldun:" He has conceived and formulated a philosophy of history which is certainly the greatest work of its kind that has ever yet been created by any mind in any time and place" (Toynbee 1956:372).

This strong convergence between these two civilizations on the high importance of knowledge and science should legitimately *discredit* the often taken for granted stand of the theory of 'Clash of Civilizations' .The Muslim and Western civilizations have clearly a solid common basis for rapprochement and solidarity. What is certain in this regard is that Arabs and Muslims are today strongly attracted by Western civilization because of its command and lead in all fields of modern knowledge and science. This factor is extremely important for today Arabs and Muslims to promote the spirit of dialogue with the West and not to clash with it.

THE POLITICS OF CONFLICTS AND TENSIONS BETWEEN THE WEST AND ISLAM

In modern times, the tensions between them are largely of *political nature.* Huntington himself has referred to this:"…however, the age of Muslim wars has its roots in more general causes. These do not include the inherent nature of Islamic doctrine and beliefs…The causes of contemporary Muslim wars lie in politics, not in seventh-century religious doctrines."(Newsweek, 2001-.2002:9)

There is no question today that the Arab and the Muslim world's hostility toward the US is strongly caused by the Bush administration often unconditional support for Israel against the Palestinians, the invasion of Afghanistan and Iraq. All signs could make one easily predict that the relations between the Arab and Muslim population and the US will take a positive radical change If the US and the West in general adopt, on the one hand, an even handed foreign policy toward the Arabs and the Israelis and, the other hand, stop the occupation of both Iraq and Afghanistan. The true adoption of that policy by the US and the West will certainly convince all sceptical persons and create a genuine dialogue between American/western culture/civilization and the Arab Muslim culture/civilization.

REFERENCES

Bochner, S. (Ed.). (1985) *Cultures in Contact.* Oxford, New York: Pergamon Press.

Dhaouadi, M. (2005). The West's Difficulties for Dialogue with the Muslim World (in Arabic). *Journal Hewar Alarab, I*(6).

Dhaouadi, M. (2006). *Culture in the Social Science and the Islamic Perspectives* (in Arabic). Beirut: Dar al Kitab al Jadid Ltd.

Huntington, S. (1993). The Clash of Civilizations. *Foreign Affairs, 72,* excerpts in the book: *The Globalization Reader* edited by F. Lechner and J. Boli. Malden/USA, 36-43.

Newsweek Special Davos Edition. (Dec.2001-Feb.2002). p.9.
Saadi, M. (2006). *The Future of International Relations: From the Clash of Civilizations to the Humanization of Civilization and the Culture of Peace* (in Arabic). Beirut: Centre for Arab Unity Studies.
Toynbee, A. (1956). *A Study of History*. London: Oxford University Press.

Index

                                    Index